Thurbe

MW01126432

Young Writers' Studio

"Don't get it right, just get it written."—James Thurber

Every other week, local teens gather at Thurber Center to write, create, and explore ways to get their stories on paper. Whether writing is a passion or just a hobby, we invite any student in grades 9–12 to join us for an opportunity to spend time with others who also like to write.

With Columbus College of Art and Design professor Robert Loss, we challenge students to take a different spin each session through exploratory exercises designed to inspire out-of-the-box thinking. A portion of each workshop is set aside for young writers to bring in their own writing to be reviewed and discussed by their peers in a creative and nurturing environment. Students who prefer not to bring in work learn how to talk about writing in a constructive way while helping fellow writers improve their pieces.

Sessions take place on select Tuesday evenings from 6:30–8:30 p.m. Young Writers' Studio is held at **Thurber Center, 91 Jefferson Avenue** (next door to Thurber House).

Each session is $15 and can be paid at the door or in advance by registering online. We also have several scholarships available for students who would like to attend.

Summer Dates 2019
June 4, 18
July 2, 16, and 30

Special thanks to our generous sponsors: Greater Columbus Arts Council, the James W. Overstreet Fund of The Columbus Foundation, and the Ohio Arts Council

Flip the Page

Central Ohio's Teen Literary Journal

2019

Columbus, Ohio

Flip the Page is a not-for-profit literary journal designed to promote the work of teen writers while providing them with experience in submission, critique, editorial design, and publication.

Flip the Page
Thurber House
77 Jefferson Avenue
Columbus OH 43215

ISBN: 9781095651162

Typefaces include:
Courier New, Calibri, Adobe Garamond Pro, and Verdana

(Front Cover)
Dark Past *by Thessalia Stephanou*
Arts & College Preparatory Academy

(Back Cover)
the nuclear fallout *by Julius Skestos*
Wellington School

Dedication

Flip the Page dedicates this journal to the wise and hilarious James Thurber, who said: "Laughter need not be cut out of anything, since it improves everything."

Acknowledgments

This journal would not be possible without the support of Thurber House, which publishes *Flip the Page: Central Ohio's Teen Literary Journal.* Listed on the National Register of Historic Places, Thurber House is Columbus's downtown literary center and a museum dedicated to humorist James Thurber. As a nonprofit organization, Thurber House depends on the support of our amazing donors. **Last year, grants and donations helped Thurber House reach over 3000 Central Ohio students through 50-plus creative writing programs** at schools, libraries, community centers, and Thurber House. *Flip the Page* is one of these excellent programs.

As always, the stellar staff members at Thurber House provide assistance. First and foremost, **Elizabeth Falter** is our flawless Assistant Editor. She oversaw the submissions process, handled communications with writers and Submissions Committee members, tracked every piece, and partnered with Editor Katherine Matthews to construct and format the journal. Elizabeth also transformed student artwork in our beautiful cover and section title pages. Without Elizabeth's talents, we would *not* have a journal.

Other awesome staffers include **Anne Touvell**, Deputy Director, who advised on this year's switch to InDesign for production. Additional assistance came from **Meg Brown**, Director of Children's Education and **Leah Wharton**, General House Administrator. *Flip the Page* appreciates the support of **Robert Loss** and **Young Writers' Studio**, a teen writing workshop sponsored by Thurber House. Young Writers' Studio provides the launching point for *Flip the Page*.

The *Flip the Page* Submissions Committee deserves a standing ovation. This group of high school writers read and reviewed hundreds of submissions. They carefully critiqued the pieces and chose the very best and most interesting ones for the journal. The Committee also handpicked the artwork and advised on the design process. Thank you for your time and opinions: Belle Walkowicz, Abby Taggart, Julius Skestos, Diana Skestos, Zizi Roberts, Mabel Mattingly, Olivia Loudon,

Grace Lawson, Allison Kuck, Anna Kennedy, Sam Horner, Haden Fulkerson, Abbey Elizondo, Samantha Derksen, Kaya Ceyhan, Defne Ceyhan, Panya Bhinder, and Alli Aldis!

Special thanks to the 2019 Columbus Arts Festival and the Word Is Art Stage Committee. For the past seven years, the *Flip the Page* writers have been invited to perform live on the beautiful Riverfront in downtown Columbus. For many of our writers, this is their stage debut. The *Flip the Page* performance always draws a big, enthusiastic crowd at the Festival.

Flip the Page **appreciates ALL the teachers** who encouraged their students to write creatively and submit their work to our literary journal. You are absolutely essential! We depend on Central Ohio teachers to spread the word about *Flip the Page*.

Special congratulations to the 43 schools and 52 teachers whose students were accepted for publication this year: Nikole Abate, Kelly Anders, Kathy Arnold, Jordan Beck, Maggie Biroschak, Seth Bixler, Bethany Black, Jenny Brooks, Carl Bucher, Brianna Butler, Todd Cecutti, Heidi Clark, Nancy de Leon, Catherine Dison, Frank Doden, Laura Garber, Sara Hardin, Terry Hermsen, Riley Hoelzer, Sara Hric, Matthew Hysell, Sidney Jones, Marie Kennedy, Amanda King, Steve Kucinski, Kim Leddy, Gary Liebesman, Sarah McCarty, Joseph McLaughlin, Bryan Miller, Leah Miller, Patricia Miranda, Tiffany Murgatroyd, Lorrie Oiler, Stacey O'Reilly, Michael Park, Fawn Parks, Abby Pavell, Paul Pflieger, Todd Phillips, Chelsea Poole, Beth Reifeis, Chris Robbins, Lisa Roberts, Aaron Sherman, Gen Smock, Brandy Spears, Renee Stevenson, Ann Trotter, Dameion Wagner, Sarah Welsh, and Kelsey Wright. Our top teacher this year was Brandy Spears with 13 acceptances. Kudos to the ten other teachers with multiple authors: Kim Leddy (4), Dameion Wagner (3), Abby Pavell (3), Laura Garber (3), Jenny Brooks (3), Stacey O'Reilly (2), Leah Miller (2), Sidney Jones (2), Sara Hardin (2), Seth Bixler (2), Jordan Beck (2), and Kelly Anders (2).

While *Flip the Page* focuses on teen writers, we also highlight the work of teen artists on our cover and section title pages. Their beautiful work makes *Flip the Page* into a book with both words and pictures. **We are grateful to our artists and their teachers,** especially Katie Owens at Hilliard Bradley High School, Melanie Holm at Arts & College Preparatory Academy, Melissa Maxson at Big Walnut High School, and Mabi Ponce de León and Helma Groot at Bexley High School.

In addition, we would like to thank **ALL the individual donors and businesses that assist Thurber House**. We are so grateful that you recognize the importance of promoting creativity, literacy, and the literary arts.

Finally, we want to thank all the writers, ages 13–19, who submitted their work. We read every piece, and we are grateful for the lessons you teach us and the beauty you share. We admire your bravery and your creativity and your talents. If we had enough pages, we would publish you all.

Contents

I. The Hitchhiker's Guide to the Galaxy

II. The Graveyard Book

III. Through the Looking Glass

IV. Brave New World

V. The Fellowship of the Ring

VI. Invisible Man

VII. Pride and Prejudice

VIII. The House on Mango Street

IX. The Time Machine

X. Walden

XI. Fables for Our Time

I. The Hitchhiker's Guide to the Galaxy

The Hitchhiker's Guide to the Galaxy
by Douglas Adams, 1979

Although best known as a humorous, surreal, irreverent science fiction novel series, *The Hitchhiker's Guide* began as a British radio show in 1978, which Adams novelized into a best-selling book, which led to more novels, a stage show, a comic book, a television series, a video game, and a movie. The main character, Arthur Dent, becomes a reluctant intragalactic adventurer following Earth's destruction by aliens.

At one point, Arthur realizes, "He was wrong to think he could now forget that the big, hard, oily, dirty, rainbow-hung Earth on which he lived was a microscopic dot on a microscopic dot lost in the unimaginable infinity of the Universe."

(Previous Page)

Views of the City *by Kaitlyn Morrison*

Big Walnut High School

2

Far from Home

I come from a place
That has beautiful nights
Full of fireflies that would decorate the sky.
While the moon glistened up above
Children would still be outside
Chasing around those fireflies.
The adults sitting on the concrete sidewalk,
Talking about the dusty roads
Made of rock
The night went on
And the wind got colder,
They finally decided to go back inside
The tall grass would shift its tips
To where the wind would blow
And in the morning
Banana palm trees would give their fruit
While lilies of the Incas open up
I come from a place
Not very well known
But still home to many of us
It will never be forgotten
No matter how far I go.

Giselle Sustaita

Genoa Middle School

3

A Little Island, Almost Like Greece

Boat rides in the bright blue ocean
Taking us to tall mountains
And old cars

Hotels with no elevators
And winding hallways
That were easy to get lost in

Little brown geckos on our windows
Stray cats on the stone paths
Leading to the restaurant we ate at daily

The same place
But different meals
With fat dogs walking by the windows

There were gift shops
And pizza places with arcades
All at walking distance

With rented golf carts
That almost drove us off cliffs
But gave us the view of a lifetime

All on a little island
Almost like Greece
That I would love to call home

Rosalie Heath

Genoa Middle School

Editor's note: A **travelogue** is an autobiographical account of a traveler's experiences while exploring new and interesting places. Famous travelogue writers include Mark Twain and Rose Wilder Lane, the daughter of Laura Ingalls Wilder.

The Heartache and Not the Front Stoop

The leaves fell on the house, resting in the gutters, on the
stoop, turning gray at his feet, there was no noise, there
was no need for any. Crumbling, yellowed, tired. As
he had expected it to be, it had aged. She died in
a car accident, intoxicated. Hadn't eaten her last dinner.
His father left the house that night.
Walked right down the front stoop.
The house still resembled what it once was, a facade of a darker life.
He stood on the front lawn with some hope, but instead
watched his father walk down the front stoop all over again,
reliving that night on a loop in his mind.
>Which way did he go?
>Left. I think.
>Did he take any of his things?
>Maybe. I don't know.
>And he didn't drive.
>No.
>Because she had the car.
>Yes.
>Okay.
>Are you going to find him?
>Probably.
>There was a man with her. Do you know who that could've been?
>No. He died too?
>Yes.

That house became the home of an older couple, they lived out their
   lives there.
Watching the years turn over from the front stoop, their rocking chairs
   side by side.
After them, a young couple. After them, a single father and his three kids,
the pavement stoop a canvas for sidewalk chalk. After them, it sat vacant.

How do you separate a house from a life?

Places become canvases for all that is felt,
and sometimes all that is remembered is the place.
It's a battle to recall the laughter and not the movie theater,
to recall the regret and not the grave,
the heartache and not the front stoop.

Audrey Molnar

Upper Arlington High School

Summer's End

Time bleeds slow through desperate hands as summer comes to a seemingly instantaneous close. The kids on Todoeswell Street cling to summer heat like reptiles, hurriedly pulling on mud-caked shoes to the chagrin of their apron-clad mothers, rushing to one another with plastic baskets full of chalk and star-cut peanut butter sandwiches. The old Planta Parque, covered in rust and overgrown grass peeking through playground mulch, shrieks with effort as kids' fragile hands pull on its aging metal, joyous laughter filling the once-abandoned clearing. The older kids of the neighborhood shake their heads in unified superiority, racing to the movies with their chore list's meager coin-count to buy staling popcorn and fizzy drinks. Erin Willard, a strawberry-blonde movie clerk, watches the summer's dragging warmth go by longingly in the air-conditioned lobby, the smell of salt nearly overpowering the scent of heat billowing from the constant flow of the movie theater entrance doors. *Ding*, they ring cheerfully, mocking Erin as she's forced to restock the ice machine. How she wishes she could put on her new yellow flower-covered rain boots her mama got in the back of the clearance shelves for her 17th birthday and go down to Abigail Hersman's backyard creek with Gregory Townhouse and Isabel Hogue, skipping rocks along the water like it was covered in sunset-colored plastic wrap until her legs ached from holding her up and her cheeks hurt from smiling. How she wishes she could visit the end-of-summer festival in the center of town run by classmate Taylor Hall, prideful in her yearly-worn purple dress and white flats, helping her friend Kelsey Wilson with her apple pie booth and competing in the eating contest, wearing a bright red chin and a dazzling blue first-place ribbon.

Despite her dreaming, there she stayed, in a morose green polo and khaki pants, serving teenagers in summer tops and flip-flops with a plastered-on Lincoln Center Theater and Arcade smile, desperately waiting for her shift to end.

The summer was falling away in strides, the drive-in movies and park adventures growing frequent in many's last attempts to show summer its true worth. Parents shake their heads jokingly while making pints of lemonade as hordes of kids from Todoeswell Street rush up to their porches in between basketball and bicycles, chalk drawings and creek escapades. The life of summer screams vibrant in passing, held desperately close near its end as everyone in the small neighborhood comes together to the largest backyard, bringing small tokens of charity. And as kids catch flickering fireflies with glass jars, as teenagers set up projectors with the latest film taken from the movie theater under the diligent thievery of Erin Willard, as adults set out plates of seasonal delicacies, summer breathes its last sunset out into the air, oranges and pinks and reds like a watercolor painting.

Summer is coming to an end on Todoeswell Street.

Grace Lawson

Heath High School

Suburban Seasons

I come from the suburbs.
The driveways all surrounded by trees
And filled with chalk drawings.
I come from cookouts
And waving to the nice neighbors.
The broken backyard swing set
And "The Big Rock"
Would be protected by fireflies
Each summer night.
Summer would be a time for
Ice cream, sweat, and flip-flops.
Winter would be a time for
Watching your breath in front of you
And wondering what would happen
If you walked on that frozen pond.
Endless winter nights always started out
With a pastel sunset.
No matter what season,
The neighborhood remained
At peace.

Brooke Middleton

Genoa Middle School

181

When I realized I lost my water bottle for about the thousandth time, I figured I left it under my seat in Room 181, where I spend about a fourth of my time during the school day. I went to retrieve it before the final period of the day, and I entered through the back of the descending, four-level room surrounded by instrument lockers. Luckily, I saw my bottle right where I expected it to be. As I walked over, I glanced up at the three loose, rickety fans hanging from the high, white ceiling, as they spun around making a light *tap tap tap* sound that a friend once told me was always at 90 beats per minute. I looked over the top of all the neat layers of chairs, each one angled to face the piano in the center. I noticed I was alone, accompanied only by those three fans, quiet chatter from distant classrooms, and a flood of the lush, vocal harmonies I had been a part of in that very room over the past three years.

I tried to imagine all of the voices that had bounced off the walls over the years. As overwhelming as that was, I realized I had come across a beautiful moment of silence in a place that has been a home to such audible wonder. In my head the various songs I sang in the past flew by me so quickly that it was nearly impossible to simply grab hold of one so that I could just listen and enjoy. I allowed my mind to bathe in the ebb and flow of musical expression, suspension, and resolution, each voice filling a critical role in the sound being produced to fill the empty space of the entire room. I remembered the music of not only myself, but of my friends as well, reflecting on the chords as a whole, not just my own part.

Nobody was around, and nobody interrupted me. No one would ever hear what I had heard. Still, I knew that Room 181 was not somewhere loneliness dwelled, for I recalled the many friendships and personal bonds that had grown simply because someone else also decided to join choir. In middle school, I was mocked for *actually* singing, but now, after years of growth and experience, I no longer feel that fear every time I walk into class. Not only do my fellow singers provide support, kindness, and joy through every note and chord, but the iconic, glorious room itself gives me a safe haven where I feel no need to limit expression of myself, no reason to hide my passions. That perfect combination of people I love and a room I feel safe in reveals a home I can walk into that never fails to remind me of what matters most, no matter how miserable I felt upon entering. I finally understood that all last year, I had depended on this room, on these people, on this music, and I didn't even know it.

When the E-flat bell rang, a long shiver ran through my body, either from 181's twenty-degrees-lower-than-it-should-be temperature or the rush of emotion that overcame me. I grabbed my water bottle and headed back to the inferior 168. I paused only for a second to consider a final glimpse before leaving the room until the next day. I quickly gave in (willingly, I might add) and let my eyes do a quick survey across the room. Once I was sure that every high-hanging acoustic panel was where it was supposed to be, I felt satisfied and left the inaudible music for the next wanderer.

Garrett Gilliom

Upper Arlington High School

The Accident

After donning long hair for several months, I suddenly and unexpectedly became the bearer of a new cropped 'do. This haircut (well, more so the events surrounding it) has thenceforth been ominously referred to (solely by myself) as The Accident. No, it wasn't a bad breakup or any other emotional reasoning that led to this decision. Rather, it was a matter of life and my scalp that occasioned me to lose several inches of hair. The consolidated tale is I was rappelling down a building, I got stuck, and I had to be cut free. The long story is as follows.

Every year, the ROTC does a training exercise in which the cadets must rappel down a flat building. Because they are sociable and manipulative people, the exercise is also open to civilians throughout the day. In fact, one outgoing ROTC student utilizes a megaphone to coerce passersby into participating. As a tour guide at this university, I knew this event was approaching, and that it could provide ample clout. I had a tour later that afternoon, which would be passing by that very location. How cool would I look if I told my tour I had jumped off that very building no less than three hours ago?

The answer is not very cool, because I would not be giving a tour that day due to the emotional trauma that occurred on said building. (In fact, several other tour guides advised me to save my tour groups this horror story, as it was likely bad PR. One day, I will frighten an incoming first-year student with this story, but that day hasn't occurred as of yet.)

Despite my chronic clumsiness and a class to attend in one hour, I decided to take the ROTC up on their offer. It is probably not surprising that I wasn't particularly good at rappelling down the building. I had to attempt the scaled-down practice session three times (thrice more than average), and it took significant convincing to get me to jump off the building in the first place. (Okay, so you have to literally walk off the side of the building *backward.* It was scary, thank you.) However, nothing is more damning than my first folly—I did not tie back my aforementioned long hair. And it was windy.

Quite simply, I started (poorly) rappelling down the building, held aloft only by a pulley system of two (2) ropes and one (1) harness. I looked behind me, as instructed by the kind army man guiding me down. Then the wind blew my hair into the ropes and tangled the two together. I soon realized that the more I tried to rappel down, the more hair got sucked up into the rope system. One more foot downward and I would have been scalped.

So, I politely informed the various ROTC officers of my situation. "Uh, I'm stuck," I said.

"No, you're fine, keep going down, you've got this."

(They seemed to believe I was psychologically stuck. That was not the case.)

Once we were all on the same page—my hair was caught, I was close to being scalped—I was instructed to stay very still, and they would be sending down someone promptly.

Let me tell you, the definition of the word "promptly" is very different when one is dangling from a building. However, eventually a strong forty-something army man—married, I later learned—rappelled down next to me, lifted me to relieve the pressure off my hair, and hacked away at the hair until I was free. He did offer to attempt to save the last few pieces stuck in the rope, but I elected to hack every bit attaching me to that godforsaken building because I wanted off of it, immediately. I then made my journey down, to meet the horrified faces of my friends and fellow students on the ground.

This haircut may possibly be the only haircut to have been done on the side of a historical, collegiate building with a pocketknife (and tidied up later, with safety scissors in a dorm room, #cheaphaircuts) in order to ensure the livelihood of the human being attached to the hair. Unfortunately, there is no saved video or picture of me stuck to said building, so I did not make it onto *Ellen*. Honestly, that was the most disheartening part of the experience. I mean, that girl who burned off her hair with a curling iron made it onto *Ellen*. I WAS STUCK ON A BUILDING BY MY HAIR. Apologies, I digress.

However, I do get some minor satisfaction when telling this horrific story. When people comment on my newly shortened hair, I say, "Thanks, it was a tragedy," and then I gleefully regale them with this very tale.

Andrea Gapsch

Ohio University

O-H-I-O

I come from warm summers
Rays of sunshine on my face
Lying out at the pool
I come from cold winters
Immediate chills when I walk outside
Hats, mittens, and cozy socks
I come from cornfields left and right
Mazes of it
Tractors plowing through them
I come from camping in the woods
Building a fire and sitting around it
Staying warm inside the tent
I come from the view of barns everywhere
The rocky ride on country roads
Riding in the pickup trucks
I come from seeing all the beautiful animals
White-tailed deer in the woods
Cardinals in the trees
I come from a white Christmas
Not having to leave the house
Looking at the beautiful snow
I come from football tailgates
Watching the game on a big screen
Scarlet and gray

Kennedy Mahoney

Genoa Middle School

On the City Bus

He's looking at the window, but not out. He's looking at his reflection, straightening his tie, combing his hair back with his fingers. Perhaps he's on his way to a date or a job interview. He meticulously disperses strands of hair as if there is a specific arrangement that will guarantee him that job or a second date. Maybe he's really on his way to his own court hearing— or maybe a business meeting or a sales pitch? His nail biting and fidgeting show me he's nervous. Nervous for what? I'm thinking through possible destinations via this city bus when he catches me staring at him. I feel my face flush as I turn away, embarrassed. I divert my attention to my own window. But, like my friend on the other side of the bus, I'm not looking out of it. I'm looking at myself. Are my fellow passengers wondering where I'm headed? Even though I'm on my way home, what assumptions can they make when looking at my messy hair and tired eyes? I find myself picking cat hair off my skirt and straightening my blouse. If these people are going to judge me, I better not be seen as a bedraggled, crazy cat lady. Annoyed with myself for being so self-conscious, I look away, and my eyes catch a person across from me and a few rows up.

Her hair is neatly tucked into a bun, and she's clutching her Gucci purse protectively. She's perfectly put together: red fingernails, designer outfit, a rock of a diamond ring. My gaze reaches her face, and I realize that not all of her is pristine. A tear falls down her cheek, before she quickly swipes it away with a tissue. Her bright lipstick is smudged around her mouth, and her lips tremble as she tries to compose herself. What put a crack in the porcelain doll that sits in front of me? Why ride on this bus and not in a chauffeured limousine? The bus begins to slow to a stop. The woman gets up and heads toward the apartment building outside. There goes that evaluation. A part of me wants to follow her, ask her what happened. I realize the ridiculousness of the thought, and I begin to scan the vehicle, searching for someone new to study.

I think back to the man I began with: Mr. Job Interview/First Date/ Court Hearing. He's drumming on his knee now, a quiet beat coming from his earbuds. I strain my ears to listen, trying to pick out the tune. It's upbeat, cheerful. Maybe a pump-up song. Is he on his way to a gig with his band? Is he a celebrity rock star and I don't even know it? Then, he pulls the string above the window, requesting his exit. The bus stops, and the man strides out, a spring in his step. Wherever could this stranger be headed? I watch him as he walks down 42nd Street, and before I know it, I'm not only following him with my eyes but with my feet. I'm speed walking toward him—bounding down the crowded sidewalk, nearly tripping over myself. Where are you going? What song are you listening to? How interesting is your life? I yearn for his answers and his story: how exactly he got to this point in his life, why he's in the crazy city of New York, what he *wants*.

He turns into a Starbucks, and almost waking from a dream, I stop dead in my tracks. Where am I? Why am I chasing a stranger down a street? Why did I get off two stops too early? I interrogate myself, as if I don't know the answers to my questions. As if I don't intrude in the hypothetical lives of others to escape from my own. To escape from my fate where the city bus will take me. To pretend that I'm going somewhere other than home—to a job interview or a first date. Even though I'm just going home, where a frozen dinner and a night alone await me. Where the same old evening becomes the same old day tomorrow and the day after, waking up too early to get to a job that I hardly care about, where I mindlessly fill out paperwork alone. And then, there's my commute.

Every day, there is someone new, someone with their own story and their own world riding alongside me. And in their eyes, I could be anything: a mother, a friend, a teacher, a writer. I could be a struggling artist or a grad student or a secret serial killer. On the city bus, my life is no longer the one I know. It's the one I hope the other passengers dream I have.

Ellie Kahle

Grandview Heights High School

Editor's note: An **interior monologue** captures the thoughts of a character. Sometimes, interior monologues can take a stream-of-consciousness form, as in James Joyce's *Ulysses*. Other times, the monologue has more structure. In this case, the narrator mixes the two styles.

Sea of Colors

I could never stay here forever. The vibrant colors would become too familiar, and the hidden figures within my imagination would no longer exist. I wouldn't enjoy the brilliant collage of colors and shapes surrounding me. I would hardly notice a rosy pink popping out from an electric blue. I would never remember the scent of the paint's oil filling the air. I would reach out and touch the rough canvas surface enclosing me, but it wouldn't mean much. Everywhere I glanced, I would not care that there are little images being masked by the big picture. When I turned right and saw a smiley face painted against an ocean-blue background, I would feel no emotion at all. If I looked up and saw a sunflower with golden petals and a vibrant red center, it would be pointless. If I brought my attention forward, and I noticed a multicolored gumdrop with a pinkish hue, it would bore me. I wouldn't even appreciate the childlike hint of a melted crayon art portrait, like the ones you make in elementary school.

My memories would show me how happy I used to feel as I existed inside this blurred rainbow. I would be reminded that I used to witness black shadows as they danced around me, and they caused colors to become bolder. I should leave before the beauty fades, and everything I have observed is gone. Before there is nothing left in my mind but the childish illustrations trapped within the frame.

Abbie Baxter

Grandview Heights High School

Magic of the Fountain

Mensa boasted the title of 16th-best fine dining establishment in New York City. The building itself encompassed some of the most unusual architecture in America, including a fountain in the very middle of the restaurant. The fountain featured live mallard ducks that swam and quacked for the amusement of the restaurant patrons. Mensa also featured a 257-year-old palm tree, whose ancient dark green leaves scraped the top of the nearly 40-foot-high ceiling. The walls slowly curved upward to form a dome, much like that of a church or cathedral.

The restaurant featured exactly 27 tables, each one covered with a thick, black tablecloth, on which was placed polished cutlery made of sparkling gold. The floor was constructed of glass-like, ivory-white marble that contrasted beautifully with the rich squid-ink black of the tablecloths. At the very top of the domed ceiling sat a circular glass window, only one foot in diameter, that let in a beam of sunlight that traveled in a circle around the fountain. Two-foot-long bronze Roman numerals were molded into the white marble around the fountain. When a beam of sunlight fell on one of these numerals, the bronze would dazzle and shine with metallic radiance, indicating the time of day like a sundial.

Waiter Yorick Larson was a few moments away from completing his 66th day working at Mensa. As Yorick cleaned the bread crumbs off the last table of the night, he heard the unexpected echo of a door slamming in the distance. He looked up, startled. As far as he knew, he was alone. Everyone else had left around midnight, and it was currently 1:14 am, according to Yorick's Series 2 Apple Watch. He could only hear the babbling sound of the water from the fountain. Slightly shaken, Yorick returned to the bread crumbs of Table 13. As he picked up a particularly large piece of stale pumpernickel, the babbling fountain suddenly ceased.

Yorick glanced about the restaurant in alarm. Was someone else in the building? Could it be a robber? He slowly put down the rag he had been using to scrape the bread crumbs off the table and stealthily began to walk toward the kitchen door, hoping that whoever was in the building would not notice him. As he walked, his footsteps echoed like hooves on the smooth, hard marble, *clip-clop, clip-clop*.

After several tentative steps toward the kitchen, Yorick saw a sudden flash of light erupt from the Roman numerals surrounding the fountain. He stared in disbelief as the bronze numerals lit up simultaneously. The light from the numerals dazzled and shone with the color and brightness of a bonfire. Yorick stumbled backward several feet, visibly trembling in terror.

The entire restaurant was completely silent, yet the lights were flashing brightly, casting their bronze-tinted light across the faded, dusty walls. Suddenly the lights stopped, and an eerie quiet blanketed the restaurant. Yorick stood for a moment in utter terror, and then he bolted for the kitchen doors, not bothering to look back.

To this day, no one really knows what happened that night at Mensa. Some say it was ghosts; some say that poor Yorick had simply had too much to drink. But whatever the cause, one thing can be said: what happened that night was *magic*.

Julius Skestos

Wellington School

Editor's note: **Specific facts** can be an excellent tool in any type of writing. Good facts make a piece of writing more interesting, believable, and powerful. Generalizations almost always weaken a piece of writing.

II. The Graveyard Book

The Graveyard Book
by Neil Gaiman, 2008

Orphaned as a toddler, Nobody "Bod" Owens is adopted by ghosts, raised in a graveyard, and gains supernatural talents that allow him to visit other people's dreams and turn invisible. Unfortunately, the same awful man who murdered his family is still hunting for Bod.

This scene comes at the beginning of the book: "The toddler's room was at the very top of the house. The man Jack walked up the stairs, his feet silent on the carpeting. Then he pushed open the attic door, and he walked in…The real moon shone through the casement window…He could make out the shape of the child in the crib, head and limbs and torso…Jack leaned over, raised his right hand, the one holding the knife, and he aimed for the chest…and then he lowered his hand. The shape in the crib was a teddy bear. There was no child.

The man Jack sniffed the air…The child had been here."

(Previous Page)

Nobe *by Thessalia Stephanou*

Arts & College Preparatory Academy

Going Toward the Light

The basement's dust hung like an ancient cloud as Nigel swiped the remaining particles. He inspected the book's unfamiliar title and climbed the stairs.

Mr. George Fairel, who sat in a worn chair, continued to blankly face the window as Nigel entered the sitting room. Through the glass pane, Nigel saw a hawk disappear with a squirrel, but George sat unaffected.

"What did you find this time?" George asked.

"I don' know. It's thick and real old. *A Trade of Sense*, it says," Nigel said.

"Who wrote it?"

Nigel scanned its front and back. "It doesn' say."

"Ah, I'll know it when I hear it."

* * *

The next day, Nigel read a few more chapters to George.

"I can almost picture it in my mind. I haven't felt that in decades," George said. "The book does sound familiar. I just can't place it. Bring it here." George ran his fingers across the cracked leather, and then the gold foil letters, as his old, empty stare persisted toward a blank wall. A sudden seriousness showed in his brow.

"I should get goin' for my game tonight," Nigel said, getting up.

"I'll have a check for you tomorrow."

Nigel thanked him. Angelina, George's wife, led him out. Nigel saw her scowl at his holey shoes as she shut the door, and he walked home.

* * *

Nigel leapt toward the basket, pushed down with his leg, and extended his arm upward. Someone slapped his wrist as he released the ball. A whistle. Nigel stopped and looked where he was.

He didn' even need to foul. The lay-up wouldn' have gone in. Why am I suckin' tonight?

Nigel stepped to the free-throw line. The ref bounced the ball to him, and he squared himself to the hoop. Black dots began to swarm his vision. Nigel shot and blinked his eyes. The ball hit the upper corner of the board, and an opposing player to his right snickered. Nigel looked at the crowd and met his mother's eyes.

What's wrong? she mouthed.

Nigel shook his head and readied for his second shot.

* * *

Nigel continued the book for the next three days. When he knocked on the door the fourth day, Angelina opened it wide enough to poke her head out and grimaced when she saw him.

"My husband is very sick and is resting," she started.

Nigel began to turn around to walk home.

Angelina quickly followed up, "Come on. He's been asking for you."

They went into the house. George was asleep on a couch, a lighted chandelier hanging from the ceiling above him. Angelina retrieved the book and gingerly handed it to Nigel. She sat in a chair across from George and sat smiling—a rare sight.

Nigel began to read out loud.

An hour later, Nigel neared the end of the story. George had woken up once and mumbled, but Angelina quickly pushed him back to rest. Nigel found it odd that Angelina reacted to nothing he read, especially from a line of dialogue he was sure she would have found scoffable.

There was only one chapter left. Black dots began to swarm Nigel's vision again, almost entirely engulfing his sight. He stopped reading and rubbed his eyes.

"All this readin' is hurtin' my eyes."

Angelina glared at him. "Keep going."

He tried continuing, but he stopped again two pages later.

Nigel furrowed his brow and held the book open in front of him. "Can ya finish it?"

"Keep going," she repeated.

And he did. But with five pages left, his eyes burned, and his vision was starting to blur. He set the book on his lap and opened his mouth to speak. Before he could talk, Angelina leapt out of her chair and jabbed her finger at the open pages.

"Finish. The. Book," she said through gritted teeth. "Finish it!" She fell back into her chair and watched George, her chest heaving.

Nigel gulped and squinted at the pages. The next paragraph took him a minute to read, and the pace only slowed. Eventually, he turned to the last page. His vision was now four times narrower than it had been earlier. Four sentences left...only three now...two...one...

He did it. He reached the final period.

And the dots covered his vision completely.

"I...I can't see anythin'."

But no voice answered. Nigel heard Angelina stifle a cry, and a squeak came from a chair as someone moved.

"George, oh, George. Honey, go toward the light."

Nigel's heart pounded and he tried to get up. He began to stand but fell out of the chair and onto the floor. "Angelina!"

"George, honey, wake up. Can you see me?"

"Yes, my love. I can see you."

Gavin Crozier

Worthington Kilbourne High School

Editor's note: To create a story with a **twist**, the writer will lead the readers in one direction by allowing them to make assumptions about the story and the characters, only to suddenly flip those expectations at the end.

insomnia

deep,
       sunken,
              eyes.
down to the bone.

dead colors,
       a fallen stare,
              slow blinking;

                   the only light
            is radiating off the TV,
       playing the same
hour-long infomercial.

       gut-wrenching exhaustion
spinning in your head.
           who knew 72 hours
               could be so long?

could any of the sex pills
       they offer
           give me
the narcolepsy I desire?

       a rotting corpse,
sullen skin,
           a milky glossed gaze;

endless,

       wailing,

           a suffering sleep
that has no wake.

Daniel Basilaia

Upper Arlington High School

26

The Curious Museum

The streets were recovering from a storm. An old man's shoes left marks on the damp pavement, and the misty morning was an unfriendly shade of gray. Thick curtains of fog hung in the air, soaked with the memory of rain. The sun was nowhere to be seen.

The museum sat on the corner of a secluded street. It was the sort of street that was only wandered during the day, for fear of dangerous somethings lurking in shadows. The old man, Mr. Edmund Smith (who preferred that people call him Ed), had worked at the museum for nearly 40 years and still remained clueless as to what it was a museum *of*. He never minded. It was a quiet and well-paying job that satisfied his needs.

Eventually, Ed reached the museum. Age had rendered the sign above the doors illegible. There were a few snakes of ivy slithering up the sides of the building, and two twisted trees stood guard on either side of the frosted-glass doors. Ed unlocked the doors and wiped his shoes on the mat within.

Inside, the lobby was peaceful. It was simply decorated and aglow with a comfortable light. There was a small desk, worn from many years of use. The bamboo floors were dulled by time. A stone fountain trickled in the corner, and a few chairs sat haphazardly around the lobby. It had been this way for quite a long time.

Ed hung his coat behind the desk and went about his usual business. He cleaned things, not because they needed cleaning, but because it was a routine, and there was nothing to do but the routine. He rearranged the chairs and set out maps, which were hardly necessary because people never seemed to need them.

The day was slow, and there were no visitors. At the end, Ed picked up his coat, ready to leave. But, for the first time, he became curious about the contents of the museum. He retraced his steps and started down the pitch-black hallway that led to the exhibits.

He used the wall as a guide until a light turned on in the first display window. Ed moved closer, peering down. There was a telescope knocked over on its side. Besides this, the display was empty. Ed felt the emptiness reflected in his own heart. Dismayed, he continued down the hallway until another light came on.

In the next display window was a grand piano. It was missing keys that you surely couldn't play without. One of the wooden legs had snapped, so the piano stood crooked. A black pen lay on the floor. On the bench was an unfinished composition, waiting for the next note.

The man stepped back from the display, confused. He kept going through the darkness, coming upon display after display of lonely, broken objects.

One was filled to the brim with sports trophies. There were rows and rows of trophies, some dull and broken, others shiny and whole. They pressed against the glass, creating the feeling that they could break through at any second. This feeling spurred panic in Ed, and he hurried to the next display.

He jogged feebly from one display to the next. A broken crib. A bent clarinet. A totaled car. He began running past the displays, going faster than he thought he could at his age. With every difficult step, the run only elongated. At last, he reached the end. The final display was dimly lit in comparison to the others and held two items.

The first was a key. He knew this key; when he was young he had used it to open a restaurant and, again, to close it for good. He could still remember the solid *click* of the lock. His fingers tingled as they relived the motion. He rubbed them together and swallowed the memory as he turned his attention to the second item—a cloth hanging from a rusty nail. It was torn to ribbons at the bottom and nowhere near its proper length. At one time this cloth had been a perfect, white wedding veil.

Ed was caught in the web-like tangle of the veil's remains, remembering the woman who was supposed to wear it. His chest tightened, his eyes flooded. His mind was tumbling, and his feet stumbled toward the glowing red exit sign. He lifted a heavy hand and pushed open the door, emerging into an alley behind the museum. That night, the stars were hidden behind a cloud, but the moon shone through the cloud. Setting his eyes ahead of him, Ed cast aside his unanswered questions and continued into the night. He wouldn't let any more of his life be captured by the museum.

Jenna Mar

Bishop Watterson High School

Out-of-Sound-Mind, *He* Takes Wicked Pride

[A discussion with the Devil]

Dearest sight-seer of my heart's attempt to beguile
Allow me this story, for in ruin I lay.
Friends boast in evils beyond measure,
If only one man were enough to take it away...

* * *

Emotion is ruin
And cannot take away the great abyss;
It boasts instead that such a thing does not exist!

Why, Am I?
Paralyzed that it might all be a dream
Is this really my face,
                                body,
                    hands,
                                        lips,
                                                        eyes?
These actions...do I own them or is it merely a clever disguise?

This room, these walls, the voice she has...how did they come to be known
    as mine alone?

By a devilish twist of the story
How am I a person? How can I boast such privilege, as this? This blessing
    bestowed on me,
Called creation.

That I—out of free will—I might choose to stand
Alone.

My body could be broken,
        at pieces in war,
        but here I sit,
        pampered once more.

Surrounded by an awakening and lack of comprehension that, while they
   might have perished,
This stranger—me, is still standing.

That which an outsider might see...
The potential of knowing—floods shock into my system.
She was beautiful. *Is* beautiful. So unlike the vile "me" manifested in a
   false mind's eye,
Brimming with life. Sweetness in the smile.
         With the likeness of meeting a small child, taking their tiny hand...
         It wells in the stomach, turning over like sand
         Standing before the picture, trying to remember the best a
            person can.

Yes.
I am real.
Yes.
I reside as this form.
Yes.
There is life after this.

Yes, God exists!

What else is there to remember in the dizzy haze that turns people
   to slaves?
And ironic it may be, it's the only thing that saves
Me.

Oh! Pit of despair
Shameful feelings of what might be real or whispers steaming from
      Lucifer's ornate mouth
That there is nothing there. Nothing beyond the sheet of religion and
      morality.
Nothing beyond the one-dimensional cloth sheening over meaningless
      existence,
Covering thousands.

"Nothing," and yet it's spewing from the tongue of a serpent.
Adam and Eve when eyes were opened...did you not think our eyes would
      overlook *your* lies?

You!
The thief of morality—
Turning brother on brother
In a silly race, pushing each other
        By *your* will "divine"
Deeper into pitiful crimes.
Joking who can "win" the most time.

Either way, they'll both die.
But I,
I will see the glory of the heavens.
Rejecting the dragon's wicked words and sly manner.
I *must* see it,
        Unworthy as I am...

You play: *"If you are wrong?"*
And...*if* I am wrong?
Believing in nothing is ignorance, believing in something a gamble.
Who does it hurt?
An ideology *you've* prescribed?
What of those who've been called to serve, love, and guide?

Shall we ring out as a chorus of
Cheers! To an industry who fears
Spinning slander on our people out of vivacious pride.

How is man to tell one thing from the other
When the rules keep changing,
Rearranging,
Devouring one another?

        There is far too much pain and suspicion
        In the World.
        Presumption of innocence lost
        Once and for all,

        hurrah.

Where will you go with what you now know?
Did you come here to gloat of your trials or confess your burning hate?
Ha!
That we might speculate and turn *you* to wield the fates?

Lia Repucci

Upper Arlington High School

Editor's note: In poetry, the **dramatic monologue** resembles
a theatrical soliloquy, in which one speaker addresses a silent
audience. In some cases, the audience is the readers; in this case, the
audience is the Devil.

The Woods

The thinnest of clouds covered the moon
And gave it a fuzzy glow
The tall grass tilted
With the direction of the wind's blow

The force of the wind caused the trees to roar
And it slanted the direction in which the rain poured
And while you'd rather stay inside during this storm
This poor girl was alone outdoors

The whistle of the wind sounded closer to a scream
The hood of the car had a moonlit gleam
If there was one wish the girl could have
It would be for this nightmare to be simply a dream

The headlights illuminated the rain-coated ground
And it lit up the drops as they came down
She got away from her car and into the woods
So she couldn't be found

Her boots squished in the ground
Struggling to stand in the mud
She tried her best to fight
The alcohol in her blood

She heard the crunch of the leaves
And she heard the sticks cracking
She heard the ground rub the flesh
Of the body she was dragging

Tears streamed down her face
There was a pain in her chest
The water hitting her hood
Drowned her uncontrolled breath

She regretted listening to the devil on her shoulder
"You don't have to wait, you had one drink," he told her
"You don't have to be completely sober"
This time he really screwed her over

This is the consequence she must face
For being the driver
Now she must cover up her mistake
And find a place to hide her

She found a patch of land
Where the body wouldn't be found
She lowered the shovel in her hand
And pushed it deep in the ground

She scooped globs of wet dirt
And made a pile to the right
Once she saw the depth of the hole
With the help of the moonlight
She put the body in and poured the dirt on the corpse
She patted the dirt, until it looked right

She looked back, past the trees
Back to her car's light
She decided not to mention
The events of this night

Freezing at the thought
She never searched for a pulse
Muffled screams from underneath
Proved assumption false

Noah Smock

Ohio Virtual Academy

III. Through the Looking Glass

Through the Looking Glass
by Lewis Carroll, 1871

In this sequel to *Alice's Adventures in Wonderland,* Alice steps through a mirror and into a land of peculiar creatures and strange reversals of logic. Alice's point of view is literally reversed as she enters the mirror world, and she spends the book trying to understand the viewpoints of the odd denizens, from talking flowers to a queen who can remember future events. Here's one example:

"I don't understand you," said Alice. "It's dreadfully confusing."

"That's the effect of living backwards," the Queen said kindly. "It always makes one a little giddy at first—"

"Living backwards!" Alice repeated in great astonishment, "I never heard of such a thing!"

(Previous Page)

Submerged *by Mackenzie Davis*

Hilliard Bradley High School

Supper

He wants his supper the way his mother always used to cook it on Sunday nights. He can still taste the lumpy mashed potatoes, the slippery greens, the cheap, stringy steak. She cooked everything too much, but it still tasted good anyhow. She said that she made it with love, and for the longest time, he believed that things like that made a difference. He figures now that it's fair enough to ask for his supper like that. So he does. He asks that everything is just a hair overdone. She said that all the time—just a hair. Sorry, everybody, the greens were in a hair too long. She was always apologizing, and he wanted to tell her not to do that, because people should appreciate that you made dinner for them, no matter how long it was in the oven.

The warden grants his request. When the day comes, he waits, patiently, for the soggy aroma of home to enter the strained space. As it comes in, he breathes in deeply through his nose. If there is anything he must capture, before his time comes, it is this. Looking at his sad little plate, he waits for home. It doesn't come. He thinks about it, about himself, about what is to become of him. He picks up his fork and swirls the greens around the plate like a child. They're limp, like his mother's greens, and smell the same. But they aren't what he remembers. He lifts them to his lips, but can't bring himself to open his mouth. He feels like he's being watched, by the whole place, by God above. He feels like he is already dead.

Will he burn? Will he see anything after his sight fails him and his body stiffens with rigor mortis? Will it be the choir, the angels, the light streaming through the melted candy of stained glass? Will it be his mother and her dimly lit kitchen? Maybe *he* will be what is cooking, like her Sunday dinner, for ever and ever.

The time is ticking down. His steak is getting cold. He tells himself that with every minute he is closer to God. He does not feel Him. He is starting to wonder if anyone has. Surely not anybody confined in this place. He tries, again, to put the greens in his mouth, to taste the last remnants of home he will ever know.

But he's lost his appetite.

Claire Schultz

Thomas Worthington High School

The Weapon of Anger

Everything is dark. No matter what, everything is always dark. Even when I'm out of the case, and He grabs me in His hands, the energy is endlessly suffocating. When He holds me, His hands are full of hate. But it's more than that, really. It's obvious that He's been blinded by it. He can no longer see any good. I know there is still good in this world, even if it may never come to me. And that is the very idea He can never seem to grasp.

His cruel energy has exposed itself for months now. However, recently it feels different. He's now reckless when He holds me. The heat of His anger is constantly at war with the coldness of His heart. His hands are a battleground, and there's a pounding tornado inside of Him. And the worst part is, I know that what He's about to do is much worse than that.

If only I could stop it.

The day that I feel the storm growing inside of His hands is the first day He has taken me out in weeks. The storm pulls me around with every scuff of His feet as he walks from His house to the nearby building, where I can hear the laughter of innocent children playing outside.

And it doesn't end until He turns off the safety.

And it doesn't end until He lifts me up.

And it doesn't end until I am face to face with a child who has a hurricane of fear inside of her.

The darkness is still for a moment, something that has never happened before.

Everything gets fuzzy as I know what is about to come next. His emotional stillness is merely the calm before the storm.

A loud crash erupts followed by a more subtle one. I recognize it as the sound of life draining.

Then come the screams. They sound like sirens that are too careful to scare anyone. And their eyes seem as if they don't know how to process that this isn't a nightmare.

The tornado is back, and it is more deadly than ever. Somehow, I can feel the last drops of mercy inside of Him being swept away. It is obvious that He doesn't want them there at all. As if that is what makes Him weak. All He wants is the winds to tear through the very children who are too terrified to even make a sound.

His finger slithers over the trigger once again. It teases and dances at a little boy on the ground. His breath is hopelessly fast. I hear the muffled screams from the boy biting down on his own sweater. The boy's eyes perch on me—the weapon that can pull his life away like the cloth of a magic trick. Every part of his body shakes as he locks eyes with a man who has no soul.

I felt the anger swirl around inside the merciless man. His glazed eyes focus on the boy beneath Him. All too quickly, His finger pulls the trigger. However, this time there's only silence. The deadly sound never erupts. The only noise comes from the crying children.

Soon His cold hands slam against me, trying to get me unjammed. The sound of Him pounding over and over is interrupted by the screams of His frustration. Once again, He locks eyes with the boy on the ground. His arm raises up behind Him, ready to strike the boy with the butt of the gun.

His hand is stopped before it can swing down. Behind Him stands a teacher who has a death grip around His wrist. With one quick motion, she pries me from His evil hands and tosses me across the floor. She wrestles with the man as she struggles to get Him away from the kids.

Not even a minute later, men dressed in bulletproof vests knock down the door and tackle the man. Kids sprint in all directions as the once-helpless boy is now protected in a crying policeman's arms. He calls him "Dad."

The girl whose fear had once swirled inside of her now rests silently on the ground, surrounded by paramedics desperately trying to save her.

I catch the little boy's eyes as he and his dad walk out the door. They focus on the handcuffed man. The very man who had a weapon of murder pointed at the boy's head just minutes before. And as I sit there studying the boy's eyes, I can't help but wonder what those eyes think of Him. Does the boy see a monster? Or does he see a man, just one who is blinded by hatred?

That boy had come face to face with a monster. A monster with me in His hands. I am a weapon of anger.

Sarah Jenkins

Dublin Jerome High School

Editor's note: When a writer gives human attributes to a non-human being or object, it's called **anthropomorphism** or **personification**. In this story, the author writes from the perspective of the gun, turning an inanimate object into a horrified observer and unwilling participant.

Sacrifice Through a Soldier's Eyes

I gazed into the dark night, hunting for VC like a cat hunting mice. Sweat collected on my forehead, my helmet pressing into my scalp. The others in my regiment followed close behind. Scanning the ground, I pointed my gun into the abyss. We walked forward slowly. Suddenly stopped by a small click, followed closely by an earsplitting sound echoing through the night, I was thrust into the air like a rag doll. Searing pain shot through my legs. Strangled screams rang in my ears. After what seemed like minutes, I hit the ground, and my arm let out a sickening crack. I rolled over, torn apart by the hidden land mine. I looked around, my vision blurred. I saw my friend just beyond me, broken beyond repair. I crawled over to him and checked his pulse. None. Tears streamed down my face, stinging the large gashes in my cheeks. I looked around for any more bodies, as I pulled the tags from his limp neck. I spotted one, his body in a ditch, charred and mangled. I crawled over to him and checked for signs of life, but to no avail. I tried to find the tags around his neck but found none. Dark figures rushed over to me. I threw my hands up defensively. They grabbed me as I weakly tried pulling my arms away. They tried to comfort me, but I couldn't hear them over the ringing in my ears. They pulled me into a vehicle and belted me into a stretcher. I heard orders barked as my vision faded entirely, with the mangled faces of those left behind haunting my worried sleep.

* * *

Sitting in the chair is the most defeating experience I've had. Lifting myself into it degrades me further. The ragged stumps that I have in place of legs continue to remind me of the crushing feeling of leaving O'Malley out in the battlefield. I wear his tags around my neck. The cool metal against my skin is the only thing keeping his memory alive. I live in an alleyway off a busy sidewalk. People rush by as I jangle my cup, waving it next to their waists. A few people drop coins into it. Some people simply ogle me, and then look away quickly to hide the obvious fact that they were staring at me. I sit there, seeing how compassionless people really are. With my sign in my lap reading "Homeless veteran of the Vietnam War. Anything will help," I wheel myself closer to the sidewalk. People continue passing me, staring at my scars or not bothering a glance. The meager earnings of today clatter into the bottom of the cup, showing how much America doesn't care for its veterans, who kept them safe through

40

times of war. And all those who died? And my best friend? If he didn't die for these people, did he die for nothing?

The thought of him dying for nothing simmers in my mind. I close my eyes to clear my head. But the faces of those killed in the blast fill my vision. The soldier who I'll never know. The friend who taught a young farm boy how to hold an M2 Carbine and an M16. The faces of the men my regiment told me to leave out in the forest.

Suddenly a hand touches mine. I look up to see a young boy, well dressed, no older than seven. His lips curl into a smile as he reaches into his pocket. He pulls his hand out and extends it. In the tiny, unblemished hand is a crumpled $20 bill. More money than I've seen in years.

He holds it out to me. "I don't need it. You can have it."

I sit there. Unable to believe what this small child has said to me. I rub my eyes, seeing if I dreamt up this boy. But he is still there. The boy who has more compassion in his hand than most people have in their entire bodies. He places the bill in my cup and gives me a hug. I'm surprised at first but hug him back. His compassion fills me with warmth.

His mother suddenly barges through the crowd and grabs him. He waves good-bye as he's dragged into the surging crowd. Seeing the boy's compassion fills me with hope for the nation. Hope that my friend didn't die for nothing. I watch as the boy leaves, his warm smile leaving a lasting imprint on me. I carefully flatten and fold the bill he gave me and place it in my pocket as the sun dips over the horizon, lazily making its way past the Washington Monument. I then cart myself back into the alley, grab my book, and read until the last bit of sun fades away.

Cordelia Long

Upper Arlington High School

The Quartermaster's Lament

The sign says there's a 24-year wait for the holodeck. The waiting area is a long, dark hallway lined with burnt-out lamps and skeletons. Inside, lights are on, and the pods are glowing, still in operation. Starveling bodies, maintained by life support's last hurrah, lie motionless within them, ghostly smiles pasted across their sunken cheeks, shallow breaths fogging up the glass. I have been working for almost 24 long years to preserve the last living members of the crew that I am programmed to protect. The only things I keep running are the holodeck, life support, and the surveillance system.

After the wreck, no matter how much we screamed for rescue, no one came. It took them a year to accept that we were stranded, adrift in space. I remember when the holodeck grew crowded as every person on the ship lost hope and chased hallucination's fragile high. They packed into the waiting area like cattle and fought like dogs to reach the door. I tried to help. I did. I promise. But when the fights became vicious enough and the lines long enough, I withdrew and waited for the strongest to prevail.

The holodeck is on the ship's lowest level. When the waiting area overflowed, they started waiting outside. Outside became down the hall, became up the stairs, became the other levels, became the entire ship. When they first started overflowing, I did the calculations. If I allowed them to rotate turns like normal, they would all die in a span of months. With the damages we'd accrued and the low probability of rescue, we did not have the power to keep the entire ship running. We did, however, have enough to run the holodeck in isolation. I did the calculations. I would have saved them all had I been able, but I couldn't. It was either none of them or 20 of them, and my programming favors the many over the few. The door still has bloodstains from the riots. This was the only way.

I have been able to stall for this long, but I can't hold on for much longer. We're on our last power cells. There would be more, but the captain wasted them on emergency signals. I warned him against it; I warned him there was no one around for light-years. He didn't listen. I would have stopped him if I could. I would have. This is his fault. If anyone ever finds this, anyone at all, let them remember that it was not my fault, that I tried, that I was just following my programming. They made me do this.

I don't use the cameras anymore. I only turn them on once per day to make sure the holodeck is in order. I don't look outside at all. I haven't in a while. There is nothing for me there. Looking outside is no help. It wasn't when they were alive, it isn't when they're...not. At least they don't hunt each other anymore. At least the bodies don't rot anymore. At least my 20 in the holodeck are untouched. They are alive, and I plan on keeping it that way for as long as I can, however long that may be, however short that may be. However short they may have.

I run the holodeck at its lowest power capacity, and even that keeps my final 20 intoxicated, happy, and blissfully unaware. At a higher capacity, the pods would be running elaborate simulations of the user's choosing, but to save power and extend the sleepers' lives, I overrode the automatic settings and forced them into a simple sleep state. They are alive, and I am keeping them that way. For the next few days, they will be happy, and then they won't be. I won't be. We will spend our last days like this. Well, their last days, at least. I can always be revived. Please don't revive me. I can barely function under the weight of my forced path with a few of them still breathing. Please don't revive me when they're not. When I have failed. At least they're happy. They've been happy this whole time. I've kept them happy. I promise. I am programmed for that, too.

I can't justify wasting power on this, but I am programmed to keep a ship's log for as long as there is power available, and I follow my programming. This is in my programming. I doubt we have enough power for this. I don't think we have enough power for this. We don't have enough power for this. This will be my final entry. If anyone finds us, let it be known that the quartermaster of the S.S. Vivencia did its duty and wishes for mercy in the life beyond.

Alyssa Shulman

The Ohio State University

Editor's note: Writers of nonfiction, memoir, and fiction have used the **diary** or **journal** as a format for telling their stories. The twist here is that the diarist is an android making its last entry in the starship's log.

Judgment Day

I can't move. I am a small little egg that is stuck in a carton with 11 other eggs. Life is pretty intense, if you ask me. I have to sit around and hope I don't get picked up by "The Hand." It is a huge monster that has five legs. It uses those legs to pick eggs up. The Hand takes eggs to a place named "The Pan." It is a very bad place that is very hot, with temperatures up to 500 degrees Fahrenheit. It is so hot that no egg has come out of it alive.

The only way to go to The Pan is by an event called Judgment Day. At the end of every egg's life, there comes a day when The Hand opens the carton. On that day, it chooses which eggs go to The Pan. If an egg doesn't go to The Pan, it goes to The Trash. The Trash is basically heaven for eggs. It is where there is no pain, suffering, or fear of being put into The Pan. In The Trash, or heaven, there is a really cool guy named God. He is the greatest egg of all, and he is the one that decides which eggs go to The Pan or The Trash.

Anyway, as I was saying, life itself is very stressful, and unfortunately, I am very old. I will soon be judged by God himself, and I am very nervous. Suddenly, the carton pops open, meaning only one thing. It is Judgment Day. I slowly watch each egg get picked up and go somewhere. I am the last one to be chosen. I feel The Hand pick me up. It has a cold, clammy, grip on me that makes me shiver. It takes me over to The Pan. "Uh-oh," I quietly think to myself, "I guess this must be the end." The Hand drops me into the sizzling pan.

I hit the metal hard. The Pan actually isn't that hot. I mean, it's a lot hotter than my house, but it doesn't seem like it is going to kill me. *Maybe this is what it feels like to melt,* I wonder. Suddenly, I see The Hand reach back into The Pan. It gently picks me up.

"Let's put it in The Trash," a booming voice says. "It hasn't cracked open yet."

I do a happy dance, as I am slowly lowered in The Trash. When I am finally set down, I see him. In front of me, there is a glowing egg on a throne. A glowing egg also known as God. I walk up to him.

"Why didn't I crack open?" I ask God.

"Because I have always known that you were a good egg, and I wanted to show you the power of God. You went to The Pan, and by the power of God, you were able to survive it, because you have faith in me. So, I want to thank you for believing in me."

"You're welcome, God," I say happily.

Suddenly, I hear a voice say, "Wow, he's so grown up now."

I turn around and see my mom and my dad. Happiness floods through me, as I see my parents for the first time in what seems like forever.

"Mom! Dad!" I run into their arms. It feels so awesome, and I know that this is because I am am in the state of eternal happiness, Heaven.

Ryan Huttsell

Saint Brigid of Kildare School

The Pen

I lie on a table awaiting
the next working day
when a hand will grab me
and press me hard
against my wide, thin companions
varying in colors
yellow, white, and striped.

When the fellow besides me
flashes and rings
I am picked up
swished around
my tip feels ticklish
yet also in pain.

Please don't crush it
on the broad surface
just because
the fellow was being rude!

Every day is like this.
After a long, dark break
it suddenly lights up
and I'm worked to death
without stop. Is the meaning of my life
to wait until I'm dry
until my lifespan ends?

Others say I am lucky
to receive the honor
of working to death
they say they are
forever forgotten
forever alone
never able to feel excitement
of a short-lived life.

The vigorous hand
loves to use me
to stab down hard
on my wide-surfaced companion
as if it were desperately
trying to leave strong markings.

The various markings
left behind
from my liquids
on my companion
the help it has brought others
signal I have not lived in vain,
it is the remnant of my existence.

Judy Lin

Mosaic

IV. Brave New World

Brave New World
by Aldous Huxley, 1932

One of the original dystopian novels of the modern era, *Brave New World* takes place 500 years in the future. Genetically modified citizens of the world government are grown in artificial wombs and dosed with a drug to keep them happy and calm. While optimistic utopian novels were in favor at the time, Huxley chose to rework that popular form into a new genre that he called a "negative utopia."

Huxley made many wry observations about writing, including, "Words can be like X-rays if you use them properly—they'll go through anything. You read and you're pierced," and "Writers write to influence their readers, their preachers, their auditors, but always, at bottom, to be more themselves."

(Previous Page)

To Chris Cornell *by Gaia Cannoot*

Arts & College Preparatory Academy

Castles in the Air
with thanks to Ella Frances Sanders[1]

Streetlamps
And wet pavement.
Loveliest of damp dusks;
We dream in terms of falling stars
Gone gold.

boketto

(Japanese: the rare feat of staring peacefully into space and thinking about nothing at all.)

Notes missed
Rule kingdoms' fates.
Since when has smashed glass laced
Your smile? Have I lost you to the
First frost?

saudade

(Portuguese: a yearning for something that may have never existed or someone you miss.)

Wonder
At this lifelike
Pirouette in a crisp
Wind. I dare you to touch the sky
And fall.

feuillemort

(French: having the subtle shade of a withered autumn leaf.)

Meet me
Where the splendor
Of autumn trees ablaze
Tempts us to imagine the clock
Wound back.

mamihlapinatapai

(Yaghan: an unspoken understanding between two people, neither of whom are willing to say it aloud.)

Anna Kennedy

Homeschooled

---

1 Author and illustrator of the book *Lost in Translation* (Ten Speed Press, 2014), a volume of words that cannot be translated perfectly into English.

Editor's note: A **cinquain** is a five-line poetic form. A version called the **American cinquain** uses a particular syllable count for each line, which provides a four-line build and a resolution. The syllable counts for lines one through five are 2-4-6-8-2.

Picking Scabs

Breaking like ice on the poles
A red river bubbling up to the surface
Pulling apart to reveal
Towering cavernous walls like the Grand Canyon
It floods and
Blood drowns the surrounding skin
Sitting on the surface
Magma flowing far underneath
The cooling stone forming obsidian crystals
Hardening the darkened shell
To break like ice on the poles again

Damien Palermo

Columbus Preparatory Academy

Editor's note: A **sustained metaphor** is a metaphor that the writer returns to again and again within a single piece of writing. In this piece, geological phenomena are used to describe a scab. The elevated language also suggests that the picking of the scab is, in turn, a metaphor for something else.

Glow

She was like coal
Tainted body
Deemed unsightly
Which made her heart blacken

Because the world made it her duty
To go against what she had to offer
By demeaning the curves of her round shape
And the fire within her brain

She ridiculed herself to the point of destruction
And forced her body to give into the pain
By burning in her own disapproval
Of her darkened appearance in vain

But she came to the understanding
That she was one of a kind
Because the blemishes she viewed as foul
Were blemishes that made her stand out

So she made it her duty
To see her flaws with fortitude
By admiring her stout figure
And the cracks that made up her skin

She was like coal
Scorching hot
Glowing in the darkness
Which empowered our souls

Meghana Karthic

New Albany High School

on(c)e more

i've had a dancer's thoughts
burn through my mind like a forest.
they're only whispers, but still swallow
with romanticism and flowers.

too long i left this flame to float
alone in nothingness, untouched and
hungry, snake-like thin, the alleyways
and corridors of wards within my head.

eventually it wore me down,
as if the mere presence is not enough
to set entire worlds ablaze
(we've seen it happen before).

the ivy illness spread, growing from my head
and into my fingertips,
starting as a tango they did from time to time
a ritual filled with passion and warmth.

and when i'd stop, they wouldn't start to rot,
but only thickened in their life and pleading:
just one more move, i'd think
and let them do their thing again.

eventually, occasion grew to habit,
and habit to obsession, and once a year
i'd give it up to them when the world grew gray
and hungry for flushed thoughts.

and now, i get out the old wooden box
where locked within live those hopes,
and let them gather the dust of
months for another thousand years.

but something with the way
i feel the shape and state of mind
i know that dust will never form.
i know that one will be on(c)e more.

Riley Hysell

Otterbein University

Unscathed

unscathed   unshaved   unblamed

who will do it when there is no fame

she sits, naked in a washtub to bathe
blinks twice, tears crusted over
enraged, she quakes

replaced a face and called it evolution of character;
its undoing is by its own self, history will be erased

at the kitchen counter, a blade is a blade
the pink towel wrapped around the hair of the innocent
        fatigued scents, wafting around the lair of the belligerent
to be unwinded, the locks fall, knife cuts, wielded
        through thick tentacles,
scatters below her feet

chopped   sliced

blithe interests fleeting
in the corner a milk bottle,
replaced with white wine

sobriety withstanding,
its grip still dwindling
on the wary taste buds
of a woman long forgotten,
        never in any picture frame.

Rowan Killina

Columbus Alternative High School

Lava Lamps Are Pretty Cool

I am watching the liquids in this bottle
Drip up, drip down to the bottom
Like ink blots
I am waiting for the liquids in this bottle
To drip, drip out and stain my bedroom
To stain my walls, my floor,
To drown me in an ocean
Of pure-ly chaotic buttercream
I am waiting for the liquids in this bottle to sustain me.

I am wishing for the butterflies to come inside and take me anywhere
but here.
To make me feel
Something other than this, upset,
This stupid mind-set,
No, I cannot evade this, I'm a modern Juliet,
Destined to love, then die, and die again.

I am praying,
I am waiting,
I am—
Sophisticated-ly
Sobbing myself into disrepair.
I am watching, I am waiting
For a person that is never quite there.
I am keeping my eyes peeled right open,
Waiting for my bra-ain to dry,
So the ink can move on, stain my heart,
And leave me here to die
How I want to.

I am waiting.
I am waiting.
I am waiting for my calls to be heard,
Even a word
To reach somebody, to make them understand,
To cause anybody to reach out their hand,
Our fingers will touch,

Our voices will meet,
Our eyes will lock, and we'll move our feet,
And that kind soul will find their way to me.
They'll stain their hearts,
Forget their souls,
Feel their mind start to shatter.
But they will be with me,
That, they will see
They'll see that nothing else should matter.
The liquids in this bottle will spill all over the continents and scream,
The butterflies will migrate away from here and find themselves stuck
in a happy dream.
And I, and the kind soul,
We will both die here,
We will be happy,
Be torn together,
Yes. We'll be happy, that is all.
Because somebody will hear my call.
Yes—
I will be happy.
I feel happy.
I could be happy, that is all.

Stazi Bednarczuk

Westerville South High School

Editor's note: In **concrete poetry**, the arrangement of the lines enhances the meaning of the poem. Traditionally, the lines are placed to create an image, like a river or a cloud. In this poem, the centered lines of varying lengths mimic the sinuous liquid inside a lava lamp.

Fortune's Fantasy

I fly, on the wings of angels I rise
And the wind will carry my legacy
Now, through the darkness, I see your eyes
When I'm gone, will you keep my memories?

I know my pen will live longer than I
Ask only for my name to stay alive
Past the shroud of darkness, I will cry
Cradled in your arms, my words will survive

But while I am here, through the shadowed eve
My pen's on the paper that it will always call home
Webs of stories it continues to weave
My deepest friend, I am never alone

Though eons may pass and centuries arrive
Never farther than memories, I will survive

Katie Hejmanowski

Hayes High School

Stars

She saw stars. Stars, crawling up her arm from her wrist to the crook of her elbow. Soft skin stained with color. When one washed away, another marched into place. Planets. Seasons. Vines gripping her arm like a vice. And stars.

Spanish, science, math. Instead of dull gray on dull paper, she made herself her canvas. Taking her pens and unfurling a world of color from the tips. Scrubbing it off at the end of the day, watching the stained soap disappear down the drain. And beginning again.

Her pens were kept in a worn fabric bag, stray threads peeking out from the edges. Tug one and it might collapse. Each pen contained a secret world. Maybe one would create small flowers dotting her veins or another would line her wrists with rain. Bold red and soft blue. New possibilities hidden underneath the caps.

She saw stars, plastic stars that were on her bedroom ceiling and lit up when Daddy flicked off the lights. Stars on her ceiling, stars in her eyes, stars marching across her mind. She used to think that the stars were real, plucked right out of the sky and stuck in the freezer for half an hour, so they were ready for her ceiling when they emerged. It made her feel a little closer to the universe.

Now, she knew better. The stars were nothing but rubber. They came from a plastic package on the clearance rack. The universe was huge, and there was no getting close to it. The real stars were far, far away. The tiny pinpricks of light she spied from outside her window were really giant balls of flame.

Kids whispered in the halls. *Her parents were divorced, no, she did drugs, no, she was adopted.* She pretended not to hear. Pretended that words were like raindrops to her, simply rolling off her cheeks and splashing to the ground. But, really, they were like shards of glass, invisible and deep-cutting. The silent killers.

She's a freak. Cutting deep into her stomach. *Liam said he saw her snorting under the bleachers, no joke.* Ruby drops of blood staining her clothes. *See those things on her arms? It's creepy.* Crimson puddles surrounding her mutilated form. Why didn't they just leave her alone? Why couldn't they just move on? They sliced and shredded unceasingly. *She's so weird.*

She wished she were a bird, so she could fly away and never look back. Simply disappear with two beats of her delicate wings. Sometimes, she could even feel the wind underneath her feathers, feel air rushing past her head and over her tail. A creature perfectly designed to escape. But then, she fell back into the real world and into her real body.

But, at the end of the day, it didn't matter. She went into her own little world, letting her fingertips take control, crisscrossing and dotting her skin. It didn't matter. Nothing mattered, really. Not anymore.

She saw stars, a good view from on top of the parking garage, the place where big kids broke bottles and little kids held their mothers' hands as they were led to their cars. She peered over the edge, wondering whether to spread her wings. Take flight. Escape. The whole world looked so small from up there, yet she still felt tiny. She rubbed her wrists. *She's a freak.* And she wanted to get away. *She's so weird.* And she spread her wings. And closed her eyes.

And she remembered. She remembered stripping your wet jackets and mittens after a day of playing in snow and warming up your numb fingers with a cup of hot cocoa. She remembered plunking out melodies on the piano and trying to sing along, a little off-key. She remembered the taste of waffles, and the warmth of the sun on your back, and the feeling of soft puppy fur running underneath your fingertips. She remembered staying up past her bedtime to look out the bedroom window. She remembered feeling closer to the universe. She remembered stars.

She folded up her wings and stepped away from the edge. Took a breath of clear, cool air. Looked up at the sky. The stars seemed a little brighter.

Annie Johnson

John Sells Middle School

Ode to John

In 1975, your eyes met mine
With your lustrous hair and your denim jacket
I thought, "Wow, that man is fine"

Then, one Saturday night, I got Travolta Fever
Your eyes were beaming like the disco lights
And you became my stress reliever

In 1978, you became Danny Zuko
You greased your hair and donned some leather
And had me going wherever you go

Time has passed, and it's almost ten years later
You're looking as magnificent as ever
And I still wish you'd be my waiter

In '97, you traded faces with Nicolas and his cages
Your grace, your ease, your style
Will stay in my mind throughout the ages

In '07, you traded bodies with Edna Turnblad
Your performance was incredible
Every single detail made me so glad

Today, I express my gratitude for all that you are
'Cause you, Mr. Travolta, will always be a star

Adrianny Suarez

Encore Academy

Reynoldsburg High School

Editor's note: In ancient Greece, an **ode** was a structured poem of praise that was performed as a song. Contemporary odes tend to focus less on form and more on praising their subject, often in an ironic or humorous way. **John Travolta** (1954-) is an actor, dancer, and singer best known for his roles in *Saturday Night Fever*, *Grease*, and *Pulp Fiction*.

V. The Fellowship
of the Ring

The Fellowship of the Ring
by J.R.R. Tolkien, 1954

As the first book in the famous *Lord of the Rings* trilogy, this epic fantasy follows the long and perilous journey of Frodo Baggins, a hobbit who must carry a magical ring to a distant land. Friendship and love play a central role in the book—particularly the bond between Frodo and his friend Samwise Gamgee, whose loyalty saves Frodo numerous times.

In *The Fellowship of the Ring*, the elf Haldir says, "The world is indeed full of peril, and in it there are many dark places; but still there is much that is fair, and though in all lands love is now mingled with grief, it grows perhaps the greater."

(Previous Page)

Fifty Years of Fashion: 1950s *by Emma Friend*

Hilliard Bradley High School

vitamin D

Paint the skies
Laid my eyes
On the one and only, you.

Perfect measure
All this pleasure
Bathe our skins in the sun's view.

In the grass
Feelings last
Forever against time's feud.

Hot and gold
Our bodies glow
And our souls shine in Soleil's food.

Zack Palino

Encore Academy

Reynoldsburg High School

Fingertips

You discovered her, drenched in the rain, drowned in her pain
You see her flaws, the scars from her pain, ones she will never explain
You saw her eyes, how lifeless they were, like a flower withering
She was tired

She saw you and wondered why you took such an interest
Most people in her past used her and treated her like a footrest
She was hopeless

You wanted to say hello, wait no, maybe how's your day
Yet didn't know what exactly to say
She saw your hesitation, and she felt the same way
There was a barrier

She remembered her tragedy and shut herself down in fear of getting hurt
The words that were, at the time, on his tongue dispersed
There was tension

There was no happy ending
Fear got in the way
They both walked away in dismay
Fingertips away

Sydney Howard

Encore Academy

Reynoldsburg High School

An Open Letter to a Late Hero

Born into a society
that I never knew would reject me—
throw me out into a snow so cold
it feels like death—
I waited,
Breath bated,
for you to come along.

My image of you changed
with every passing year;
summers bygone and winters past,
all of my dreams have
led me here.
To a dull dream of who
you might be under your mask.

When I was young, you
were the prince on the steed,
Styled smile and plastic personality,
nothing about this hero seemed real.
Because it wasn't—
I just saw a Disney movie
and believed I needed saving.

As I got older, you became
a masked marauder, super-villain-fodder,
doing good for good's sake became
awaking, longing for the perfect fate.
The hero: flawed-not and
filled with ambition on a mission.
Yet a mask was all you were.

Today I've come
to this realization,
The hero that has taken
So long to save me from
my own damnation was
Me, all along.

ed up every idea,
ked like fruit from trees,
ery "dream hero" was the
pple to my Eve; and
bit from a fruit forbidden
to me.

I had to face a reality,
The reason I fell in love
with a dream hero
Was because so much
was missing from
me.

M Rigsby

Central Crossing High School

Editor's note: When a writer directly addresses a person who is absent or has passed away, they are using a literary device known as **apostrophe**.

Under the Umbrella

Black spread out, shielding us from the night, shielding us from the pitter-patter of rain that seems to never stop, the cool mist whisking across warm skin, chills shiver down my spine whenever the conversation starts again. The streets are silent, but the light still shines GREEN. More lights begin to pop up, but I can't stop to focus on the scenery, trying to keep you out of the rain and not make it so obvious that I'm loving every second I spend with you. I look away to keep from being scorned for looking too long, for loving through my eyes, you continually hurt me to remind me that you are not mine and that I can never have you. Everything I write ends up turning into a love piece about you, because I cannot fathom a life where I can't walk with you in the rain, on a street with no cars, just our voices echoing through empty alleyways, as rats scurry along around us, you jump and leave me behind because you couldn't sacrifice for me, every step you take creates a new link in the chain that I had hoped would bind us together. You, so unbothered by the touch of the rain, while I stick close to the handle of my umbrella, life is easier to handle when you have something to hold on to, but it would never be you. Brown, our skin, our eyes, with your laugh, color fades, and I am filled with a warmth that outlasts the freezing touch of the crystal-clear rain when it hits my skin, every drop making me recall a memory that is too hard to go back to, so I always look to the future; avoiding looking in your eyes, avoiding confronting a wound that would leave me devastated, that would leave me contemplating the depth of our relationship. You left me in the rain, under my umbrella, because you could never seem to sacrifice for me. Black spread out, protecting us from the cold that you are too comfortable in, Black spread out, Brown our skin, clear rain blending in, you left me, spread out in the rain, blackening under my umbrella.

Playon Patrick

Fort Hayes Arts and Academic High School

Friends

Sometimes I feel like nothing but a shadow.
I follow you, but you don't follow me. We
cross paths, but can never meet.

Sometimes I feel like you hide my
existence. You don't want the world to know
who I am to you.

Sometimes I feel like a grain of sand, mixed
in with everyone else on the beach. You
build me up in your castle, only to let the
waves wash me away.

Sometimes I feel like my footprints are gone,
and everything I've done no longer matters.

Sometimes I feel like I'm all alone. It's as if
you aren't next to me. You talk to me, but I
can't hear your words.

But sometimes I feel like a rope is pulling
me back. I hear your voice, and I smile and
laugh.

And sometimes I feel like I can't let you go.
You mean too much to me for me to say
good-bye.

But I always feel like we're friends.

Courtney Boyd
Genoa Middle School

Disinterest

Why must I yearn for the boy who doesn't care
The one with misty eyes and a constant scowl
Meant to make him appealing, but it only looks cruel
The boy who tells me he hates my books, and plays, and music,
    my cities, my home
He scoffs with contempt, and his conversations are void of empathy
Trying to prove that we are opposed to each other
If he doesn't care for anything, how could he for me
But I tell myself that I can make him, that I will open him like a flower
And his love and passion for me will bloom in hues of gold and maroon
Instead, I have found he has made me cold
We talk and my body turns rigid
My goal, to show how little I care
And I hate myself when I'm with him, because I want him, not the
    rejection he offers me
How can I care for him, long for him
If the only time we are near, I turn harsh and closed
With a cold face and a rough body
Relationships are passionate with love, and dreams, and vulnerability
All we share together is apathy

Phoebe Helms

New Albany High School

73

For A$AP Mob, with Respect to the Earbuds

That stretched across whole years/though I crushed them daily/into
my pocket/ wore them thin with 808s/shaking in my ears/like white
pebbles/on a railroad/the train/taking my hearing with it as it passed/
disappearing/for a crucial moment/just long enough for my momma
to tell me

> You're not spending all summer
> On the East Side, or wherever
> You and your little friends go
> To line your mouths with sugar
> And let all them brands I won't buy you
> Dance out, one by one

Me and my friends don't play A$AP Mob out loud;
We talk fabrics and shoe game
While background noise
Rips out of a speaker. That is enough.
All else is memorized
Punch lines which can be practiced with earbuds
And an empty room, same as anything
We do with unfazed eyes;
We are exactly who we say we are

When our pockets are full enough
We go by the thrift store in front
Of the railroad tracks that catches
The solid gold blades of sunrise
And let ourselves bloom in the afterglow
Well-trained eyes finding our reflections
In the rows of secondhand stores and stories
Waiting for us to retell them.
I take my pocket change/curating my share of someone else's words/
wrapping them around me/and even though they get tangled/I can still
hold them/like a breath/before an insult/a comeback/before the start of
a poem/like anything stolen/made into your own/and released/dazzling/
back into the world/

Tomas Miriti Pacheco

Columbus Alternative High School

The Feeling

Going all the way back to a late night in May of 2017, when I was just about to finish my sophomore year, I got the certain feeling that I needed to call up an old friend of mine. Now, if you're reading this, in an effort to make sure that my friend's identity is as anonymous as possible, I will only refer to them in a gender-neutral tone and as "Friend." But back to the point—I hadn't contacted Friend in years. We had a kind of falling-out back in middle school, but I still always cared for them. On this one particular night, a feeling came over me. It was a deep, darkening feeling. It felt like something was about to go horribly wrong. My shoulders became heavy, and my heart was thumping. Something was going to happen tonight, and it was my responsibility to stop it. I had never felt this feeling before. A feeling that some say came from God directly. I needed to call Friend.

We talked for hours. I don't even remember what we talked about, but it's not important. Then, finally, Friend revealed the truth to me. The reason why I got my feeling. The reason why I needed to call them that night. They said it. And my fingers started to float. My nails felt like they were being lifted from their beds. There was a huge lump in my throat the size of a rock. Instantly, tears came into my eyes. So many tears that I couldn't release them at first. I felt myself begin to choke. I couldn't breathe. Every word I attempted to say felt like it was being yanked out of me by someone shoving a rod down my throat and into my gut and pulling them out one by one in the most excruciating way possible.

Friend was going to commit suicide that night.

They had told me that they had already printed out a bunch of pictures from their past, lit some candles, and grabbed a razor. They were sitting on the floor, ready to begin, when I texted them. And as soon as they said that, I sprang from my bed and started getting dressed. But they told me to stop—that there wasn't any need to worry anymore. Hours of talking had helped them calm down. Despite the fact that they told me not to and that I didn't know their address, I was ready to call the cops. I wanted to send the police to their house. To break through their door and protect them. To require them to go through therapy and get help. But they convinced me that they were okay. I refused to leave them alone until that was true. Finally, a mere two hours from the time my alarm would go off for school, we hung up the phone.

In the time since, Friend has been doing better. We grew a lot closer as individuals, and it was eventually revealed to me that this was in fact not Friend's first attempt at taking their own life, but their third. But don't worry, there was been no threat of that since.

Unfortunately for us, Friend and I are no longer on speaking terms. We had a huge falling-out a couple of weeks ago. But I know they're protected. And I also know what kind of person they are now. It was a rough end for us. And I know that that's because we became too dependent on each other for everything. It hurt, getting rid of them. It hurt real bad. But now that I'm alive and free, I have never felt better.

We may not have worked together forever, but we worked together for a while. And for that while it was good. I believe that I was put in their life for a reason. For that one night. And for many nights after that, which were full of happiness and memories that I will never forget. But I never want to see them again, and I think that's okay. I think it's okay for people to only be good for each other for a short time. I think it's okay that, while we shared some of the most intimate and personal moments of our lives, we don't share anymore. And I know it's okay that, because of each other, we are saved.

Charis Ellett

Big Walnut High School

An Open Letter to a Friend

Dear The One Who Never Gave Up,

You have entered my life in a flurry of creative instances. You've lifted me to a place where I'm no longer scared of the world, and I will respect you forever because of that. There's nothing I've seen you do without a bright smile and wild eyes. You're a beacon of love and light, and you should always know that. I've never met someone like you, and my only regret is that we didn't become friends sooner.

I know you've been through a lot so far in such a small amount of time. You've been through so much heartache and heartbreak that I'm surprised you're still here. Most people would've fallen at the first sign of trouble, but you kept going. You kept loving, even if the chance of loss was higher than finding what you were looking for. The fact is, you have a resilient heart. No matter what happens, you'll always stay strong. I know you don't believe a word I'm writing, but please promise me that you'll take what I'm saying into consideration.

So listen to me, please. You are a queen inside—I know it and so does the world. All you need to do is convince the heart that's beating in your chest of the same exact thing. So, that's all I have to say. Now go. Make the world a brighter place.

From,
Your Best Supporter

Jada Wilkins

Pickerington High School Central

Editor's note: **Epistolary prose** is written in the form of a letter or a series of letters. The same is true of an epistolary poem or novel.

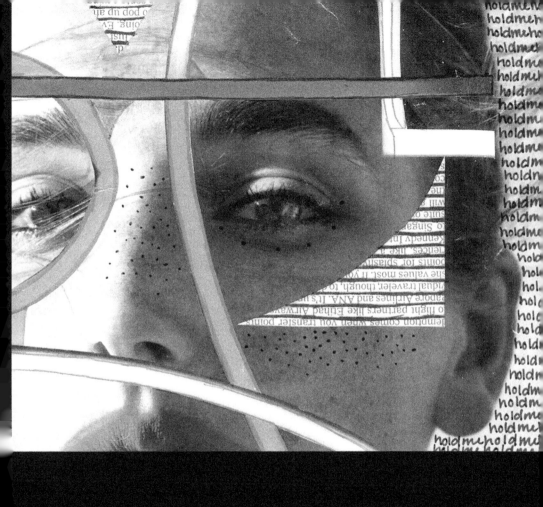

VI. Invisible Man

Invisible Man
by Ralph Ellison, 1952

Ellison's groundbreaking novel portrays the life of an unnamed African-American man in the first half of the 20th century. The man narrates the story, and his efforts to understand himself and American society take many strange turns, and his experiences range from realistic and wrenching to symbolic and surreal.

At the end of the novel, the narrator observes: "And my problem was that I always tried to go in everyone's way but my own. I have also been called one thing and then another while no one really wished to hear what I called myself. So after years of trying to adopt the opinions of others I finally rebelled. I am an invisible man."

(Previous Page)

nine *by Allie Bushong*

Bexley High School

Bad Indian

When you're like me, there's a simple way to draw attention away from your body hair or ashy knees: spicy food. If you can't fit in, just down a shot of hot sauce, and all your troubles disappear. One minute you're going to the bathroom to wet your knees, and then one spicy swig later, you're surrounded by kids clapping in amazement. Just make your way up the Scoville scale, and you're in.

I'm not in.

I'm supposed to like spicy food. It's supposed to be my quirk. My Indian blood is supposed to be 65% curry—but maybe all that curry is just clotted up in some vein.

But I love chicken curry.

I love masala dosa.

I love biryani.

I even love beef pickle.

But only if it's mild enough for me.

Is there some sort of rite of passage that no one has told me about? Do I need to wolf down a tablespoon of curry powder to activate my super-Indian-powers? It works out for everyone else; why hasn't it worked out for me? Why are Scovilles the missing piece to the subcontinental puzzle? Most importantly, will I ever find that piece?

Jaya Parail

Village Academy

Editor's note: **Irony** is a literary device that can be used to sharpen the tragedy (or humor or drama) of a situation. Irony involves a mismatch between what is expected to happen and what actually does happen.

81

The Closet

We are running down the halls, my brother and I, racing to get to the bathroom. When he shoves me into the closet, I land with a loud boom. The wind from my brother whizzing past slams the door shut. I sit for a second, thinking to myself how ironic this is, me sitting in the closet. It means so much to me, figuratively and literally.

I sit in the darkness and remember my first sleepover, which was just this past weekend.

When I arrived, I saw two girls from school and a girl I had never seen in my life. There were pizza and games in the basement, and we did that for a bit, until one of the girls suggested that we play truth or dare. I hated that game with all of my might, but I was scared to say anything, because the girl who suggested it was one of the quote-unquote Mean Girls.

All of us gathered in a circle, and we looked to the birthday girl and asked, "Truth or dare?"

Her immediate response was, "Dare."

No one could think of anything until I blurted, "Call your crush, and tell him that you like him. Well, if you like boys, I mean."

She looked at me with a glare and asked, "Who do you like?"

Avoiding her question, I shot back, "Do you really need to know?"

The honest truth was that I had a crush on her, even though I knew she could be a jerk. I loved the way she laughed and how she could make a whole room stop and stare. I could feel the tears welling up.

"I have to go pee!" I blurted out, not wanting to cry in front of them.

The tears had already started pouring down my face when I saw her mom standing in the kitchen.

She asked, "What's wrong, honey?"

"Nothing. Just girls are mean, so I can't tell them." Then, I whispered, "I don't necessarily like boys." I crossed my fingers and prayed that she wouldn't judge me for it. I stood there for a minute—then I looked up and saw that she was on the phone.

She hung up and asked, "Did you say something, honey?"

"No, but I want to go home, though," I stammered.

"First sleepovers can be hard," she said with a comforting smile. "Let's call your mom."

* * *

When I got home, I went straight to bed, feeling sick to my stomach. I got up in the morning, and my brother and I raced to the bathroom.

And that brings us back to me now, sitting in the closet, just sitting there. I stand up to leave, and I know this is kind of cheesy, but my heart is still there, tucked away on the top shelf in a shoebox.

I go out into the world, where I would have to hide from my parents and my friends.

* * *

The next day, I get a call from one of the girls at the birthday party.

She says, "I have to tell you something."

"What is it?" I respond, slightly worried.

"I think I have a crush on you, and I think that you like girls, too," she answers in a quiet voice.

Happiness rushes over me. The relief is like a flood. I don't have to be alone. I have a rock, a friend who has no secrets. Finally, I can be myself—at least sometimes.

Fiona Ike

Dominion Middle School

Pride

Suppose you just tasted the most wonderful cake you've ever had. People start telling you that cake is disgusting and wrong. Would you stop eating it because of what other people think?

Suppose you had to live every day with the way you love under fire. People will shame just about anything that's different than their twisted version of "normal."

Suppose people are so fascinated with the way you identify. Too busy passing hate to stop and even try to understand.

Suppose you must watch those whom you love turn you away due to something out of your control. They could never understand anyway.

Suppose you are one of millions who is discriminated against because of whom they choose to love.

Suppose you are told that accepting who you are and being proud is a crime, a sin.

Suppose you are able to finally accept yourself, after living in shame and denial for so long. Oh, to know what that's like.

Suppose that being considered controversial became a normal thing.

Suppose surviving every day was a struggle.

Natalie Pillar
Genoa Middle School

I'm ABCD

I'm ABCD. My parents said that all the time, but I never asked what it meant, because I thought it was some technical term for work. One day, I walked into their room, and I heard them talking about someone.

"He's ABCD," my mom said, to which my dad replied, "Really?"

I finally asked what it stood for, and I could not believe the answer. "American-Born Confused Desi." Desi means Indian, so the acronym basically means an Indian-American. I'm an American-Born Confused Desi.

I love sweaters. Every so often, though, you get that super-cute sweater that ends up having a million pieces of lint stuck to it, pieces of fabric that have been separated from the sweater but still stick to it. I'm that piece of lint.

* * *

"When you came to America, did you ever find it hard to stick to your Indian culture?" I asked my mom.

"No, but you get torn sometimes between the Indian values and what's expected of you."

What's expected of you. Whether it be in academics or sports or any area of my life, I am expected to be the best by my parents and, mostly, myself. But sometimes, my goals don't align with those of my culture. In India, there are three career options: doctor, engineer, or lawyer. However, in America, it's all about the American Dream and reaching for the stars. In my case, that's literally what I did by pursuing the unconventional field of astrophysics. When my twelve-year-old cousin asked me what I wanted to be, she was taken aback by my answer. As if she were older than me or knew better than me, she replied, "It's okay. You still have time to think."

That piece of lint is now cemented in its position, separate from the rest of the sweater.

* * *

"Were you ever scared, Mom? To come to this country alone?"

"Some days I was. I was fascinated by the culture and learned so much, but I was so far away from family. Everyone was so self-centered here. In India, it's all about 'we' as a family."

* * *

Family is the most important thing in Indian culture, but it's not valued as much here. I've grown up in a home where you always put your family first, but I started to lose that a little bit because I felt that my family was different. I felt that because my dad spoke broken English with an accent, I should be embarrassed of him.

As I was separating from the sweater too much, my dad told me a story that put me back on track. He told me about how he was also embarrassed when his own father wanted to come with him to his first day of med school, and he didn't take the time to appreciate how proud his dad was. And so, the piece of lint remains firmly attached to the beautiful sweater.

* * *

"Did you ever feel like a foreigner?"

"Of course. I mean, I am a foreigner, so what is there to feel?"

"But you're an American citizen. Do you feel like you have to work harder to prove you're just as American?"

"Yes. The combination of being an immigrant and a female is what made me feel that I had to prove myself at every step."

* * *

My mom's aunt came to one of my dance performances, and she said something that will stay with me: "You know, I thought you were a complete American, but when I saw you dance, your Bhangra, I knew you were a Punjabi girl."

In both cultures, I don't quite fit into one or the other. I may be considered Punjabi when I dance, but I won't be in other aspects of my life. As immigrants, we are constantly asked to prove our love for America. And as Indian-Americans, we are also constantly asked to prove our love for India. Lint is never considered a part of the sweater, even though both are made out of the same materials. Lint may be separate from the actual sweater, but it also can't seem to let go.

* * *

"I feel like I don't really belong in America, but I'm too American to be totally Indian, Mama."

"Why? Why does it have to be one or the other? You're Indian and you're American. I feel incredibly fortunate to have lived half of my life in

India and half of my life here in America. Indian culture will always be with you, and so will the American. You get the best of both worlds."

* * *

I don't have to take a lint roller and strip away half of my identity. I was born in Syracuse, New York, in the United States of America. I'm the daughter of immigrants. I'm an Indian-American.

Panya Bhinder

Columbus Academy

Editor's note: A **metaphor** allows a writer to describe an object, action, or concept by using an unrelated object, action, or concept. In this piece, the writer uses a humble piece of lint as a metaphor for her complicated identity as an Indian-American.

Biracial

Living life on both sides was never easy.
Not knowing where I belonged made me feel queasy.
I'm both black and white
But I couldn't choose a side to be on, it wasn't right.
In school, I was too white for the black kids and too black for
   the white kids.
What does that even mean?
Was I not "ghetto" enough?
Was I not "preppy" enough?
Either way, I'm fed up.
I don't have black or white features
And I get labeled like I'm some type of creature.
They say I don't belong
And that's just downright wrong.
It's 2018, and this is the cruel world we live in.
Tried to fit in
Bought the nicest kicks,
Used proper grammar,
And the funny thing is I didn't have to say which is which
But you understood what I meant.
I'm neither fully black or white
And I don't like needing to act like I'm one or the other to feel right
In my own skin
Because at the end of the day, I consider both races my kin.

Cierre Childers

Reynoldsburg High School

a memoir of feelings

1.
the scent of failing
the scent of growing
the voice of ignorance
the voice of leadership
the feeling of paper
the feeling of graphite
the sight of confusion
the sight of understanding
the taste of disappointment
the taste of success

all live
under the same roof
either in distress
or
in harmony

some call it hell
but to me
it is the process
of being educated
while still young

2.
imagine being called
a different name
a name that
you do not
call yourself
a name you hate
a name that
wrinkles your spirit
a name that you
cannot blame others
for calling you
because

they do not know

i wish that
you can use telepathy
to tell them
who you really are
so you will not
have to endure
the pain of remembering

3.
being like me
is painful
when you are young
because those
you know well
try to "defend" you;
"it is a phase"
"it is a joke"
but in reality
i do not need
to be defended
by someone who hurts
more
with words like those

the words of the
unknowing
and socially ignorant

4.
i still have an
unused stack of
suicide notes

i do not know
why i still
have them,

89

but i can guess
it would be
a waste of sharpie
and paper.

i write them
when i forget
that
it is a
bad day
not a
bad life

i wish i
was not so dramatic
or that i still
listened to others' opinions

5.
what does it mean
to be motivated?

it means
being able to
convince yourself
that you are
able to do something
and
be proud of yourself
for what you did

motivation is not
yelling
screaming
demanding
punishing
because
someone does not
have the energy

and self-confidence
to make something
happen

6.
i'm sorry

it's all i
have to say
nowadays

i apologize
for things
i never did

because
i don't like
to see
people angry

it's easier to
take responsibility
than to fight
for yourself

it's easier
to just be prey

7.
first
there was hail
the size of
chocolate chips
you made with
the batter
alongside mother

then

there was enough rain
to wet your whistle
well enough

then
there was enough wind
to blow away
the neighbor's mouthy terrier

i write so
while watching
prisoner of azkaban

how lucky was i

i didn't have
to work like dogs

8.
wouldst thou
dusk of apricot
be of resemblance
of the innocence
of a child

wouldst thou
witching of mauve
be of resemblance
of the slumber
of the senile

wouldst thou
clouding of sky
be of resemblance
of the lost
of an opportunity

9.
love is like
a wrapped gift
but inside
is an heirloom

somebody
gave it a name
and it has value
and in order to
keep it in
the best shape
you need to
care for it

and if you can't
you let it go

love is like
your uncle's
amethyst geode
with pegasus
perched on top
he gave your mum
before he passed away

10.
a shade of green
that wraps around
my heart
a tight garment
that introduces without words
i have waited
so long
for the only embrace
i need

i adore my binder
my chest compressor

i listen to the instructions
for washing
like a troop
and hang it
on a hanger
when it is
not being used

i care for it
like a child

it was worth
the wait

11.
you hear it
"she cut herself"
she talks about
the sister you used
to hit

why?
one says
"she was depressed"
"she was getting bullied"
another says
"her friend told her
and she did it"

so you ask yourself
and you understood why
she thought she had
nothing to lose
she was already
being hit at home
when you hit her

you were just

an infection

12.
sometimes i get sad

but then i remember
that when i write
a will
i can write
that i want
to be mummified
in
fruit by the foot

and nobody
can stop me

13.
writing stories
and novels
and poetry
is internationally considered
a branch of art

the art of putting nouns
and verbs
and adjectives
together in harmony

this is an example
of modern art

Benjamin Christian

Hamilton Township High School

Editor's note: An autobiography or biography seeks to depict the entire life of a person; a **memoir** focuses particular memories of interest or a particular period of time.

At Best

At best I'm loud.
I stand up for myself and never mince words.
At worst I'm afraid. I'm afraid to be afraid, to let my self-confidence waver
  for one second
because that's all it takes before everything falls apart.
I'm worried that I'm lazy, I fret that I'm mean, that no one really likes me.
But the world only wants flowing emotional confessionals with words of
  floral tones.
Instead I'm walled-up, angry and scared, so frustrated with my feelings
  all the words that come out when I try to explain them is a manic
  cacophony of expletives so rich and expansive, an angel loses its wings
  upon hearing it.
Perhaps it's easier to be biting. Perhaps it's fun to be quick.
But after all I'm just running from what I've convinced myself I'm not.
At best I'm a scared child who's just learned to punch above my weight.
At worst I'm a scared child who fears that's all I'll ever be.

Zizi Roberts

Homeschooled

Room 304

There's a girl in Room 304
Who cries herself to sleep
I hear her tears fall down her face
As her pain goes down too deep

She faces her fears all night
As I told myself in my mind
I can't bear to hear her suffer
From this locked door I am behind

Her sobs need to be held
Her tears need to be dried
Her thoughts need to be heard
As her heart's told to guide

Somebody needs to see
The corners of her mind
The depth of her thoughts
And the words down her spine

And as I sit and look
At the wall of 304
The door handle is pushed
And she comes out the door

I look and meet her eyes
And I finally see
The person behind the door
Has always been me

MaKenzie Hilling

Hilliard Bradley High School

13

13 is a painful reminder of past experiences and future worries.
I look into the mirror of 13 and see an anxious, sobbing little girl.
If I could go back in time and help her, I would just let her cry into
My arms.
I would just tell her that even if it seems that it is you against the world,
Take the world by storm.
Yell, scream, and do everything you can to change this
Godforsaken world.

I am the oldest child, the newest reincarnation of a generation.
I am the guardian of these feisty redheaded children,
The worried, sickly Mias.

I am now a warrior, armed with my former mistakes and victories.
I am heading into battle, facing my foes with only myself to guide me.
I am the hero in the midst of a magical journey, who consults the wise
Oracles for guidance for the future.

I wake up on a spiritual plane, surrounded by past and future versions
Of Mia.
They tell me seemingly trivial advice, along with hints, clues and
References about my life.
My life that I almost gave up six months ago.

Every time I face a mountain, I have a team of experienced climbers
Behind me, supporting me with my difficult decisions.
If I fall, they remind me that I've fallen before and gotten up again and
Again.

13 reminds me of a time gone by, of a scrapbook of memories.
Flipping through the pages, smiling at the little things.
The shirt I was wearing, the expression on my brother's face.
I can go back there, experience what happened all over again.
All by just looking at a picture.

Now my actions are not "childish," they are seen as an effect of being a
"Moody teen."
An eyeliner-clad, goth teenager.

I'm not like that, nor are many teenagers I know.
We are not children, we are young adults
Trying to survive in an adult society.
Trying to pretend like we know what to do.
Trying to navigate life.

As I sit here, listening to cheesy pop music, I wonder about my future.
I know not to dwell on dreams, but to look toward the horizon.
That horizon scares me.
Not my heart, since it knows that I will go down the right path.
Despite this,
That horizon scares me.

Mia Doron

Hastings Middle School

VII. Pride
and Prejudice

Pride and Prejudice
by Jane Austen, 1813

As a modern young woman in the early 1800s, Elizabeth Bennett is smart and witty and entertainingly judgmental. When she first meets out-of-towner Fitzwilliam Darcy, Elizabeth immediately dislikes his distant attitude and snobbish observations. Over the course of the novel, they fall in love and must admit their own failings—their prejudices and pridefulness—in order to embrace what is truly important to them.

Upon hearing that Elizabeth and Darcy plan to marry, Elizabeth's surprised father makes clear that she must be true to herself: "I know that you could be neither happy nor respectable, unless you truly esteemed your husband…Your lively talents would place you in the greatest danger in an unequal marriage…My child, let me not have the grief of seeing you unable to respect your partner in life."

(Previous Page)

Pattern *by Eleanor Rupp*

Bexley High School

A Man on Mars

Sometimes I feel like the moon.
Distant.
Always there but not always perceived.
Sometimes I feel like waves crashing onto the sand.
Flowing, everlasting.
Constantly moving, thriving.
Sometimes I feel like the wind.
Both big and small.
Consuming everything in its path.
Sometimes I feel like rain.
Pitter-pattering on a rooftop.
Loud but calm.
Sometimes I feel like fear.
Not knowing.
Not understanding.
Having everything and nothing at the same time.
Sometimes I feel like blue.
Chilling, cold, sad.
The color of everything.
Sometimes I feel like humming.
A soft noise, not appreciated.
A vibrating feeling that slowly moves through a chest.
Sometimes I feel like traffic.
Moving, but ever so slowly.
It never ends.
Sometimes I feel like the grass.
Swaying.
Underneath your feet.
You can't see me.
Why can't you see me?

Arabella Pierre

Genoa Middle School

Let It Come

The clouds they hover with no remorse,
with Dark, with dim, with gloom;
rain soaks our hair, our clothes, our shoes,
the walls of every room.
Nothing can protect us now, nothing to keep us dry,
not you, not me, no trees with branches soaring through the sky.
Nothing to protect us now, not even the crowded sun;
standing in the rain together,
I say let it come.
Still nothing can protect us and nothing ever will,
so when the rain falls down on us, we race to the top of the hill.
Our fingers enlaced, our hearts beating as one
We yell, we scream, we tell the world
We say let it come.

Bailey Schull

The Ohio State University

A Day in the Life

Arms spread and tight muscles loosen from a night's sleep.
Heavy feet glide across the wooden floor, trekking to the closet.
A hairbrush cascades down your smooth locks,
Your strong smile glistens in the mirror, and you turn to go to school.

You catch your reflection in a passing window.
Your paper-thin skin radiates little light,
For your solemn, sunken eyes reveal
The emptiness of your ever-dismal cheeks.

Grass cushions your toes as you carefully step off the porch
As to not disturb the nature at your feet.
Crouching down to the rough but inviting mulch,
You spot a vibrant purple butterfly—your favorite color.

The butterflies fluttering in your stomach evolve
To become beetles that threaten to pinch away
Any hope you were straining to hold on to.
Your face is straight, but you are numb.

Your new sneakers lightly tread the hard asphalt
As you cross the restless road of today's travelers.
Your steps fall in unison with the chaos of cars around you,
And your hand fidgets with the keys in your pocket.

Your own hand crawls up to your hollow throat.
Each finger smoothly finds its place in the grooves of your neck.
You begin to tremble as you know what's next:
A tight squeeze to suffocate your pleading cries.

The hallways gleam with bright faces
And buzz with stories pouring from every mouth in sight.
Shoulders rub against yours, but you don't budge.
The books remain balanced on your steady fingertips.

You cannot balance everything at every moment.
Worries constantly stalk their unsuspecting prey
And demand all attention like a shrieking kettle.
You know it's not too long before everything boils over.

Izzy Walther

Upper Arlington High School

Pieces

We are not the ones who broke the world
But we have no choice but to pick up the pieces

We are children
And instead of being bright and starry-eyed, we are dark and jaded

We are too young
to see the way famine ravages the world
to know that greed is more powerful than hope
to believe that hate can beat love

Yet we do.

Because the adults we are supposed to learn from
Are the same ones who spread poison through the world

So while we are trying to grow our minds,
we must cope with this harsh reality:

Our world is hateful and divided
And it is our burden to pick up the pieces

E.J. Wendt

Phoenix Middle School

Life Can Be Full of Love

Sometimes, life can be beautiful. When it happens, it's so perfect that it almost hurts. Like breathing in fresh air after inhaling smoke, gasping and smiling and simultaneously pressing a hand to the burn in your chest. So good that you already miss it before it's even gone. For children, life is full of these moments. Everything is new and wonderful and conquerable, and kids aren't tall enough yet to see above all the good to all the darkness.

Sometimes, I think about how children always have these absurd dreams about who they are and who they want to be. Untouched by pain and rejection, they aspire to be astronauts and cowboys and presidents. Adolescent veterinarians hug their rabbits, and fledgling superheroes run around in capes. Maybe life would be a little easier if we loosened our grips on the boundaries drawn for us after we grow up. To go to space, all you have to do is close your eyes, and to see beauty, all you have to do is look for it.

Early mornings in cold air, with sunlight bleeding across the sky like watercolor paint. Socked feet on kitchen tiles, boiling water and warm steam meeting spread hands to become shivering droplets. Cross-legged on a porch, feet swinging from where you sit atop a wall. Tippy toes on countertops while fingers reach for chocolate chips. Spine to the ground while elbows bruise and air struggles to get past lips parted with laughter. Popcorn exploding like stars, limbs moving to music, hands over eyes to the soundtrack of gift wrap, clumsy feet on skateboards. Somersaults, arms reaching for someone, orange lights reflected in alleyway puddles, snowflakes in hair like crystals.

Subtle wisps of dreams surround us like cool breezes. Take hold of the things that matter to you, don't wear society's judgments like a windbreaker, and you'll see so much more than you once did. Look for the things that kids find so easily—laughter, gentleness, compassion, kindness. Let these things guide your experiences instead of the expectations given to you and know that your life can be full of love, if only you make it so.

Anna Rolinatis

The Ohio State University

I Will Never Know

WARNING. This story contains mature content.

I slam the door behind me as I let out a frustrated scream through clenched teeth. I kick off my shoes and stomp into my room, not even bothering to turn on the light. Tears well up in my eyes, and I plop down on my bed.

"What is wrong with me?" I ask aloud. "Why does everyone *hate* me? Why can't I just be normal?!"

I let out another scream, this one louder. So loud that it seems to race through every room, stripping them of their innocence, their happiness, until when I stop, there is nothing but silence. I can't hear anything. Not the cars outside, not the dogs enjoying their midafternoon walk, not my neighbors having friendly conversations out their screens, the houses so close to each other that if two people happen to reach out the window, they could hold hands. Only the ringing in my own ears.

I stand in front of the mirror and strip off all my clothes until I am stark naked, looking at my body, hating it all. I stand there, looking at myself, letting the cool November air drift through my open window and chill my body. I don't move, not when my foot has an itch, not when I want to run my hands over my cold arms to unfreeze them.

This is appropriate perhaps. This is how my body will feel when all the life has left it, my mind says.

I walk, slowly, to the office. Slowly. Unlock the case. Type in the password. One number at a time. 2. 37. 10. 5. I wrap my hands around the cool metal and breathe. I know it will be one of my last ones. I walk back to my room. I'm careful not to make a sound, even though no one is home. I stop in front of the mirror once more and hold the gun up to the light. I let the sun reflect off of the barrel, let it make distorted figures around my room.

This is what it has come to. Nobody wants me. Everybody hates me. It would be better for everyone if I were no longer here. It would be better for my parents. One less child to be mad at, one less child to feed. It would be easier for Sarah and Emily at school. They wouldn't have to stick up for me all the time. It would be easier for my teachers, who keep asking about the cuts, when I've already told them I fell off my bike. It'd be easier for everyone. **I'm not wanted.**

I scream again. Again and again and again. Again and again until my voice goes hoarse and cracks. The silence that was once peaceful is now suffocating, and I'm choking.

"I'm sorry!" I shout, my voice raspy. "I'm sorry that I'm even here to begin with!"

I'm not even supposed to be here anyway! My parents didn't mean to make me. It was a one-night thing. And my mom? The only person that truly loved me left. Left for that job in New York. Promising to come and visit, but then she got herself in that car crash. I wasn't even allowed to see her body. Wasn't even allowed to hold her hand one last time. I betrayed her.

"SHUT UP!" I yell. "Shut up! I know I'm not good enough, I know that nobody wants me. I know! I know!" A strangled sob comes from within me, desperate for release.

I put the muzzle on my forehead. It's cold, just like my skin, and I almost don't feel it. But then, it's more sudden. I'm startled about how normal this feels. I click the bullet into the chamber.

I don't know if death will be better. I don't know. But it has to. It has to be, because nothing could be worse than this.

My voice drops to a whisper, so quiet I can barely hear myself. "It has to be better."

And my finger squeezes the trigger.

* * *

I will never know how at school tomorrow, everyone will be wearing black. I will never know that the whole school will have an assembly in my honor. I will never know how they said my name, over and over, *"Iris, Iris, Iris."* I will never know how much Sarah and Emily cried when they found my body, broken and cold, just like I had predicted. I will never know how much my aunt and uncle cried, how devastated they were. I will never know a lot of things. I won't know because I am dead.

And there is nothing.

Annie Wendt

Phoenix Middle School

Sometimes: A Collaborative Poem

Sometimes I feel like I never want to grow up.

Sometimes I feel like my childhood is flashing before my eyes.

Sometimes I feel like a skydiver without a parachute.

Sometimes I feel like I can do anything, as long as I set my mind and my heart to it.

Sometimes I feel like I have been buried alive in a hole, dug by my own guilt.

Sometimes I feel like a piece of laundry folded away in the closet. I am forgotten about until I am needed and put away again.

Sometimes I feel like a book that never gets read, collecting dust as time goes on.

Sometimes I feel like I only dream in black and white.

Sometimes I feel like I have been hit by a truck as soon as my head leaves my pillow.

Sometimes I feel like homework, unnecessary.

Sometimes I feel like just another leaf on a tree, in a vast forest.

Sometimes I feel like it will get better. Things will improve. Times will get better.

Jordan Alloway, Aiden Chao, Sidney Choo, Tracy Darius, Sandy Ilangovan, Beckham Parsons, Gwen Reed, Talya Roper, Shannon Wyatt
Genoa Middle School

Editor's note: This **collaborative poem** contains the voices of nine writers. Each author wrote their own poem using the same "Sometimes I..." format, creating an opportunity for a multi-voice piece.

Forever

There are some people in life that you think are going to be there forever. You'll picture a thousand different versions of your future and they're in every single one, like it's not even a question whether they'll be there or not. You'll trick yourself into believing that you have it all figured out because young love is blinding, and you're more than just a kid now. Your mind is so easily convinced that the amount of time you spend with someone is some type of promise, and that it will always be like that.

One day you realize forever is never promised. You are struck with a wave of pain, and you are reminded that you were wrong to believe that everything would stay the same. You crack under the pressure you placed on yourself to hold things together. Your brain comes undone, spilling thoughts onto concrete floors, pouring sadness into the hands of those who know how strong you are. You are enraged at your mind for allowing you to even dream of a future that was certain.

Eventually this will pass. You will recollect every broken piece of yourself and turn it into art. You will come to understand that you can't control what the future holds and trying to do so will leave you empty. You will see that just because they didn't know how to love you, it doesn't mean you are unlovable. You will find your worth within yourself, not from promises they couldn't keep and words they didn't mean. Forever is never promised and that's okay.

Jolie Rapavy
Dublin Coffman High School

Every End Is a New Beginning

Amy Sutherland is the worst, I think, as I keep my eyes glued to the rock I have been kicking for the last ten minutes. *How dare she "accidentally" put MY diary under the document camera?*

It was projected to the whole class on the TV, opened to the page where I wrote about Brayden, the most perfect human on the planet. That is the reason why she is the worst.

I approach a crosswalk and look up at a street sign that reads "Campbell Dr." Raindrops start plummeting down on my head. I hate walking home from school in April. I look right, then left, and decide it is safe to cross. I continue to kick my rock.

The roaring of a car's engine is drowning me before I can even turn. Its impact squashes me like a bug.

My breath thins.

My head throbs.

My ears ring.

My eyes are blinded by the brightest light I have ever seen.

Every emotion I have ever felt swarms me like bees around a hive. My life is flashing before my eyes. My brother Lucas is screaming, my mother is singing in the kitchen, my dad sighs at the TV screen, probably watching football. My best friend Emily is laughing. Amy Sutherland is laughing at me.

Then, everything is gone, and it's just the blinding light. I feel as though I am nothing. My body is gone. I'm not alive. I'm gone. I'm dead.

"Abigail Edwards, you have completed your first life," says the voice of what I assume must be an angel. The voice is fresh, new, and not like anything I heard while I was living. "Prepare yourself to be born again, but as Peter Evans."

Everything and everyone I love is floating away like a balloon in the sky. I'm the toddler screaming and crying and jumping to get it back. My life is going away and away, until it is like a dream that you remember less the more you think about it.

I'm crying. I'm screaming. I burn with the pain of losing everything. The only thing that is left is the bright white light.

It all stops. I am in someone's arms. She is crying. I am crying.

"Hey, Peter. Hi, I'm your mommy," she says. Her smile outshines her tears.

I'm Peter, and she is Mommy.

Devin Mitchell

Saint Brigid of Kildare

VIII. The House on

The House on Mango Street
by Sandra Cisneros, 1984

Teen Esperanza Corden lives in a small red house on Mango Street, in a Puerto Rican/Chicano neighborhood in Chicago. Her family is close-knit and poor, and she must wrestle with many challenges, including racism and assault. Esperanza tells her story in vignettes that often feel like poetry.

Esperanza brings her family to life by comparing and contrasting their hair: "Everybody in our family has different hair. My Papa's hair is like a broom, all up in the air. And me, my hair is lazy. It never obeys barrettes or bands. Carlos' hair is thick and straight. He doesn't need to comb it. Nenny's hair is slippery—slides out of your hand. And Kiki, who is the youngest, has hair like fur."

(Previous Page)

Bloomington *by Eleanor Rupp*

Bexley High School

Crossed Toes

For as long as I can remember, I've crossed my toes, the large over
    the small.
I don't have a reason for it, it doesn't make sense,
But I do it.
There's a picture of me as a child, when my hair was still blonde, and a
    bowl cut covered the top of my head
And in the picture, I look out,
Away from the camera,
Away from my hands that wrap my father's head as I sit on his shoulders,
Away from my mother who stands in front,
Away from their loving smiles and crooked teeth.
Though I was in the picture, I wasn't there at all.
Somehow, I had already moved on from their happiness,
Their eventual divorce.
Those eyes that searched some object out of frame knew the future,
Because they had seen the outcome before.
Those young eyes are ancient, old as the scaly king of the swamp,
    old as its oldest ancestor and old as the salty soup of stars that
    birthed all life.
Those eyes, my young eyes with their infinite potential,
They ponder. I see them processing, even in that snapshot of time,
And I see my feet
With their crossed toes, intertwined like fingers which hold knowledge of
    my gifts:
Then observation, now poetry.

I see that I knew, even then at that young age, exactly what I needed
To give back to the world.

Elijah Lothrop
Columbus Alternative High School

115

The Two Best Parts of Me

There is a woman
Who always stands tall,
Who fights her own battles,
And who does not take "no" for an answer.
Her car is never back in the garage before seven,
The only time she's at the stove is on Christmas Day,
And it takes her ages to find something in the grocery store.
There is a man
Who has lines of laughter around his eyes,
Who says things in a way that makes you remember them,
And who others imitate when they're trying to do the "right thing."
He's never late,
He doesn't know how to commit with anything less than his whole heart,
And he takes pride in cooking dinner each night.
There is a girl
Who walks with her head held high,
And sprinkles laughter around her like confetti.
She knows just because you're up late working
Doesn't mean you shouldn't still be early,
And that the only person who can put limits on her
Is herself.
She'll keep looking for a way
Even when you tell her there isn't one
And she lets her conscience lead her
Down the straightest path she can find.
The girl hopes that one day
She'll be able to teach her children
Just half
Of what the woman and the man
Have taught her.

Emily Dewolf

Columbus School for Girls

116

Grandmother's Red Chair

Grandmother's red chair lingers
In the living room, and
A duster rests on its arm—
Forgetting to dust years ago.

This wine whispers denial;
Its bottles line her spice drawer—
She had vied for thyme but grabbed merlot.
Tired, retired, she resides in her chair.

This ominous mass mildews me
Like a 50-year-old oak waiting to grow and
You've truncated my 60-year pain and
You've ruined my life, she says, and
I'd rather collapse into my chair than be here, Jeanette says.

Her wisdom has waned like the ennui flavor
Of old porridge. The taste of old platitudes once
Comforted but now numb like raw ginger;
I wish for hugging matriarchal wisdom—lost
From a forgetful red throne.

Jake Lord

Upper Arlington High School

Randy

I have spent so much of my time trying not to think about my grandfather. It is not because I hate him, for I have my mother's blood pumping through my veins. I am not allowed to hate him; I am only allowed to love him, so, therefore, I do. There is both too much to say, and also nothing to say about Randy Rudisell. German lineage wraps its way around his wrinkled, round face, and his body weighs down on him in the same way that his past as a southern Baptist preacher weighs down on me.

I love him.

His thin, gray eyebrows are saturated with distinct, individual hairs that create a pathway to his hollow eyes. Eyes that haunt me in a way that I do not fully understand.

I love him.

A thick, bright orange Oklahoma State University polo shirt encapsulates him, tightly, like packaged meat. A polo shirt that perfectly exemplifies his tasteless, southern pride and stubbornness.

I love him.

His laugh is loud and booming, but short-lived like a hushed and rusted church bell. He reminds me of something I want to forget in the same way that I remind him of the most precious thing he has ever lost: Sherry Rudisell, his daughter. I loved her.

I love him.

Ever since her flame went out, his will to live has become nonexistent. His hollow eyes are in a state of constant longing and grief. When he looks at me, he sees her. A way that I never want to be seen at all.

I love him.

His laugh propels me back eight years, and I am small in a pastel-green house with shiny, hardwood floors and five rooms that, at the time, were big enough for me to lose myself in. A light brown, glossy piano sits in the living room, which is washed with pale sunlight magnified by the large window that overlooks a Texan's front yard. The grass is dead and lifeless, and the sun is unforgiving. He makes me see her. Over and over and over and over and over again. I'm sure I make him see her. Over and over and over and over and over again. Her small, slim figure laughing when he laughs. I am forced to carry her with me. He is forced to carry her with him.

I love him.

Every time I see him, I feel repulsed. A man who used to carry my small, young body around on his robust shoulders is now a man who cannot stand to look at me anymore. For my mother's blood is pumping through my veins. I often wish that I could rid myself of her gnawing presence, but her button nose has found its way to my face, along with her angel dimples and incessant smile. To look in a mirror and see someone who is forever lost is as heartbreaking as having to look at a granddaughter, a child who should bring you joy, and only feel a gnawing presence. He forces me to apologize for my existence. I force him to apologize for his decaying mind, as dementia washes its way into his already deformed and broken brain.

I love him.

However, I am devastated to admit that his now-lost eyes are easier to face in comparison to the eyes that would often look away when I entered a room. His eyes that would shed tears when he would speak to me candidly about how similar I am to my mother. It would produce the most horrific taste of bile, clawing its way into my mouth. His lost eyes only occasionally present pure grief. Sometimes, he'll wake up and think that her flame had never gone out, and he will be stabbed with the eroded, repetitive, dry news once more.

I love him.

I am just terrified that he will see me and then see her, and then I will have to see her. This is why I no longer call, why we never visit them, why they never visit us. One day, I will look into a warped mirror, and I will be heartbroken when I see his soul looking back at me, knowing that I could have done something to rebuild a bridge of grief-stricken screams and tears.

I love him, but I still can't stand it when his hollow eyes look into mine and he calls me by a name that has stained every room I have ever walked into. When he calls me *Sherry*.

Chloe Gonzalez

Mosaic

Through My Eyes

Brother	Sister

Brother

I have a sister

My god, she's annoying

All she does is whine

And those friends

Gossip, gossip, gossip

Hey! That's mine

Are you kidding me?

pause

I never thought I'd miss those sounds

Taking the good moments for granted

I HAD a sister

It was just supposed to be a quick run up the street

Sister

I have a brother

My god, he's annoying

All he does is eat

And those friends

They smell!!!

Stay out of my room

MOM?!?!

REALLY?!?!

pause

I never thought I'd miss those sounds

Wishing I could take back the bad

I HAD a brother

Mom sent him to the store

Something we've done time and time again	Something we've done time and time again
	But this time
Things were different	
I did everything I was supposed to do. I was supposed to go home that night	He did everything he was supposed to do. He was supposed to come home that night
BANG	*BANG*
Mr. Police Officer	Mr. Police Officer
	Can't you hear the cries of a young girl whose heart you have stolen
Mr. Police Officer	Mr. Police Officer
Can't you hear the silence fill the air from another life you've stolen	
More memories were in the making	More memories were in the making
	He was gonna teach me to drive
Beat the guy who broke her heart	Send me off to prom
I wanted to be a college graduate	You watch the news
You listen to the radio	
I never thought this would happen to us	I never thought this would happen to us
So from here	So from here
I will guide and protect you	

From here	From here
	I will march in your name and all the others
Wishing this pain on no one	Wishing this pain on no one
	My brother
My sister	
I love you	I love you
	Come home to me...

Ka'Leea Reditt

Mosaic

Editor's note: **Poems for two voices** are designed to be performed by two people. The text appears in two columns, one for each speaker. The poem is read like a conversation in verse, with the readers taking turns. When the poet wishes both readers to speak at the same time, she positions the words on the same line in each column.

Great Papa's House

Pulling up the driveway,
All cracked, bouncing on the potholes.
Getting out of the car in the big garage,
Wondering why he needs so much space.
Hear the sliding door screech,
As you pull it open to walk in.
Immediately you smell it,
The smell of furniture sat on for decades.
First thing you see, the kitchen
With its old cabinets and the squeak they make when they open.
As he welcomes you in, he opens the fridge,
Every time you come, you know you get chocolate milk.
As you walk back in the house, you pass furniture,
You pass the grandfather clock,
Hearing the dingdong every hour, on the hour.
Into the bathroom you go,
Taking in the old tile and woodwork.
And you smell it again,
The wonderful smell that makes you feel at home.

Caroline Dietz

Genoa Middle School

2nd Family, 2nd Home

I remember the dirt
Stinging my eyes
Clogging my throat
Even when I screamed for my teammates to score
Hair baked by the brutal sun
White shirts and pants brown
Blisters on my hand from holding a 22-ounce stick
Blisters on my feet from running around and around
I remember the tears
Some good
Most bad
Stinging my eyes like salt in a wound
Getting lumps in my throat from a hard loss
Or even smiling through the tears
Congratulating the other team
Slapping hands
2nd place doesn't feel great
I remember hide-and-seek in the hotel
Giggling with my teammate who became my family
Looking out on a brown field where I spent my childhood
2nd family, 2nd home

Lillianna Burky
Genoa Middle School

Worth Life and Worth Death

My father always said there are only two ways to read a book. There's the just-getting-by way, skipping your eyes across the page and picking out words that look important. That's how you're supposed to read manuals and biographies, just getting the gist of the information, 'cause that's all you need. Don't tell Mama, but I read all my school books that way.

The second way is how my father reads his classics. *There's a soul in books*, he would say. *A soul you only hear if you read it with your heart, not your eyes.* 'Course, I was only 11 and couldn't understand how my heart could read a book. But he loved his old books, loved them until their spines peeled off, loved them so their pages were dog-eared and the ink faded and the paper crinkled. When I was sick and couldn't sleep, my dad would sit on the edge of my creaking bed with one of his books open. He read the words aloud, his voice like a stream trickling over rocks, caressing each word with a cool and steady touch. He spoke of young men with dreams to fulfill, good criminals, and cruel benefactors, 'til I fell asleep to the cadence of his voice flickering the candles in rhythm.

When I grew older, I tried to be like Pops and read his books. I was 13, so I thought I knew all about the intricacies and palpitations of the heart. I was determined to find the soul in the books, the soul he admired most.

But my eyes found only words on those pages. Instead of reading, I would study the stains between the lines, smudges that could be dogs or trees or geese or anything, anything to make me feel the words were something more. I felt helpless when I read his books, like a blind man trying to figure out a painting. How could I understand the soul in the books when the words weren't meant for me? I had no place in his books.

I told him as such late one night, as we were watching the stars gleam over the fields. I told him about the smudges in his books and the swimming in my head.

But Pops leaned over and set his hand on my shoulder. "My books are my books. You have to find one that speaks to your heart."

His answer was as elusive as the others, and I wanted to tell him so, but with his hand gripping my shoulder and dark eyes seizing mine, how could I speak?

I remember his eyes again at the worst of times. Years of his love culminated in a portrait of my father lying in his bed, sweat dripping off his nose, cheeks as white as sheets, amber eyes swollen and watery. My mother's voice carried from the light in the hall, speaking low.

I knelt beside my father, his most beloved book on my knees. My voice shook as I tried to read to him, more a trembling bush than his running creek. I fumbled over the name "Pip," and my father reached out to me, his hand tilting my chin up.

I could read every tear that fell onto his pillow, every tremble of his lip. My father, my papa, the strongest person in my life, was broken and weak. His clammy hands told my cheek this wasn't a break that could be fixed, a sick day willed away by spoken word. I could barely breathe.

"'You are in every line I have ever read,'" he whispered, and closed his eyes.

My father died when I was 15 years old. He left behind his work shed, his dog, his wife, and his books. Those old, dusty, dog-eared, broken books. To this day, I try to find what he saw in those grimy pages. I run my hands down the cracked spines, I devour every word, but I don't feel his touch or his impassioned gaze. If these pages hold any soul, it's the soul of Pops, his calloused hands, and seeping voice, the way he held Mama in the kitchen, the look he gave me when I was moments before sleep, how he gazed at the stars each clear night.

Now I'm here, my childhood long gone, holding the book he loved more than anything in this world. And all I can do is picture him beside me. Is this what you wanted, Pops? I'm trying to find a soul in your book, but my heart can't read when you aren't around. Every word, every letter makes me think of you. You taught me everything I know. But without you, there's only one thing I always seem to remember.

"You are in every line I have ever read."

Allison Kuck

Canal Winchester High School

IX. The Time Machine

The Time Machine
by H.G. Wells, 1895

A science fiction story from the Victorian period, *The Time Machine* follows the wild adventures of a scientist who invents a time-traveling device and journeys to the far future.

Wells once said, "We all have our time machines, don't we? Those that take us back are memories…and those that carry us forward, are dreams."

(Previous Page)

Invention *by Kaitlyn Morrison*

Big Walnut High School

Broken Chains and Freedom Tracks

Life wasn't always the best on the farm.
But even though we weren't free, we were together.
At least not until that day. I saw a white dove,
reminding me to not lose hope in a better future,
such as a seventeen-year-old would do.

It's the year 1823, five years after little Janie's death.
I take out the secret picture that little George Lockhart drew
and secretly gave to me. It is of Janie.
I push the memories back, as deep as my mind would will it,
whilst shoving the crinkled paper back into my tattered pants.
"Malkum!" a low harsh whisper can be heard from the cook, Maddie,
   a fellow slave. "You can't have that out! What if you were seen? Then
   the plan would be ruined."
Her eyes scream fear, but no other signs of emotion show.

We are getting out of there, tonight.
There is a train and nothing to hold us back.
Benjamin Lockhart is one of the most feared slave owners in Georgia.
He is a cruel and heartless man.
But there is a supply train coming,
and we are going to ride it all the way to the North.

We go through the day acting normal,
so they don't see us slowly packing some food and water and
   gathering blankets.
A little girl dropped a jug of wine in the kitchen today.
This changed something, because she was left in the barn until nightfall to
   be punished.
When word spreads to me, I know we have to take her with us.
But it could sacrifice everything.

I shake it off until nightfall. When we are almost to the tracks,
near the farmhouse, I hear a sob. I look to Maddie,
whilst I hear the last words of my parents, just before they were sold:
"Stay strong, and don't fight unless you're looking for death."
But I have to fight. I couldn't save my sister, but I can save her.
Maddie nods. I dash into the farmhouse and see the girl.

129

There is a rope tied like chains around the child's wrists.
I finally break her free and hear shouts from behind.
I never look back.
I just run to the tracks.

Sara O'Neil

Genoa Middle School

Peaceful

I used to find it peaceful, sitting and staring
Overlooking the vast plain of grass,
Wheat,
All mine.
I'd sit on my perch, the fence post
Watching the cattle graze,
The tractor plow through the wheat
Moving slowly with the wind,
Leaving a trail of fresh, dark soil in its tracks
Feeling the sun lazily warm my back,
But it is all
Gone.
Like a quick hare, the dust came
Dashing through my plain of wheat,
Devouring everything in its path
Effortlessly sweeping my hard work
Away,
like a broomstick on our front porch
Turning the sunny day into night
Replacing it with a storm,
A dark blizzard.
I watch from a window,
As the cattle are smothered, slowly buried
By the black cloud,
Viciously howling with the wind.
Descending on them like a swarm of locusts
Tearing away at grass.

I find it peaceful,
The silence after the storm.
There is nothing here,
No wheat,
No wind,
No grass,

Only dunes of parched soil from far away.
Just a desert.

It is peaceful.

Madeline Lyons

Genoa Middle School

Editor's note: **Depictive historical writing** uses the tools of fiction or poetry to recreate a historical event or experience for the reader. This poem, like the two pieces that follow, depict experiences from 1930s America—the Dust Bowl and the Depression.

The Dust

Living this life, out in the plains
Everything is covered with a layer of dirt.
We live our lives day to day,
Fearing that it might never end.
I'm growing up, but not how I want.
Instead I'm standing here in the barren fields
Waiting for the next storm to hit.

Looking through the clouded glass,
Breathing deeply through a wet cloth.
This morning I saw nothing,
Just black when the sun was out.
The black blizzard approached,
So we prepare for the night,
Despising the life we live.

Today, I hear droplets on the soiled roof.
The first rain in a long time.
I believe it's a miracle but,
The downpour is the opposite.
The soil, washed away, just like my hopes,
I have to get away from here,
Before it's too late.

I no longer want to hold the overused cloth,
I want to breath the fresh air of the coast.
I am leaving this plain, and my life.
I've been told of how it used to be.
I will touch the ocean, smell the flowers,
I will listen to the birds and taste, oh taste,
Anything but the dust.

Allie Strosnider
Genoa Middle School

I Am God

On the windowsill I sit, a book perched in my hands, and satin tied to my head. Sunlight pours through the tall, white windows, projecting dainty squares on my face. Coffee's scent fills the house, and the walls surround me. They rise up and over me like a mother. I look down toward the streets. I'm the king, and the windowsill is my throne. There are many other gods, peering from their windowsills, and we sit in solidarity.

I look down and watch the child collapse on the street corner. Her brother is quivering in desperation. He panics frantically, begs for assistance, but no one does anything. You can't blame them though; you can't help others when you have nothing to offer. When you're up here in heaven, life is blissful, but below it's a battlefield.

You can see the fear in each doll, each wage cut, each hourly cut. Faded coats, faded smiles, faded spirits. The man bawls, the woman weeps, and the boy cries. The bull has failed them all. I wish I could do something but I am only god.

Elizabeth Mauk

Genoa Middle School

An Empty Field

Another turning gear in the city that never sleeps, Alexander worked as a technician, maintaining the computer systems all across Wall Street. Every day, he would come to work on the same bike, ignoring noise from the same people and entering the same gray buildings. Here, he would labor away, working floors below people richer than him, trading stocks of companies in which he couldn't afford to take part. Alexander felt he was an underappreciated factor in Wall Street, the heart in a sedentary human, slowly withering from denial.

Stuck in a constant cycle of work just to pay for a run-down apartment and rotting food from the gas station, Alexander would have an epiphany.

It was the winter of 2008, with the gray skies weighing down on him, Alexander would enter the building he had been assigned to, walking into a room of panic. The date was December 30, and the housing market had just witnessed the largest price drop in its history. People shouted, printers spewed files, and noise flooded the room. He worked through the day, under a steady stream of pressure from the constant noise. Even after work, he made his way through panicked crowds of stockbrokers, financial advisers, and defeated investors. Alexander's head ached, and his feet were blistering from pacing around the dimly lit computer rooms of Wall Street.

That night, he got in his car and drove, with no specific place in mind. His only objective was to leave. Leave the tense stock exchanges, the greedy landlord, and the taunting loudness of the city, slowly driving him to madness.

Behind the wheel, his head descended and rose slowly, as he tried to stop his conscious from giving into sleep's tempting pull. He could no longer stay attentive and simply began to let his muscles naturally direct the car along the roads. For hours, the car moved and turned along roads as if driven by a ghost, one moving entity in the darkness.

* * *

Rays of sun shone through the clouds, waking Alexander. He was beside the road, still in his car, with the engine still running. Looking in all directions, he saw nothing but a straight, paved road, fading into the distance with no car in sight. The gas was drained, from both driving through the night and a continually leaking tank. In a tired stupor, Alexander slowly emerged from the car to the scent of fresh, untouched air, the opposite of the city air he had breathed for years. On both sides of the road were fields of wheat blowing in the wind, void of human contact. Flipping open his phone, he gazed at the "no cell service" marker. In another blow to his mentality, Alexander simply walked into the field, for he only required peace.

With the dry wheat crunching under his feet, Alexander felt calm for what felt like the first time since he had moved to New York. Such a simple field it was, yet it was a much appreciated gift bestowed upon the busy man. He lay down, wheat obscuring even the faintest piece of humanity, his car, and the road. It was as if he and the blue skies above were having a one-on-one therapy session. For hours, Alexander stared as clouds moved by slowly, a juxtaposition to the rushed business associates flooding the floors of stock exchanges.

Alexander, once a man trapped in an unsatisfying cycle, had found peace. Not just amongst the fields of swaying wheat, but within himself. Even if he never came back, even if this location never existed except in his mind, he could imagine it and feel peace. Perhaps, he never reached the location, instead falling asleep at the wheel and running the car into a ditch on the night he attempted to drive away from his problems. It was during the ill-timed slumber he would encounter such a therapeutic place.

Yet, as he stumbled back to his apartment, leaving his car in the ditch, he felt at ease, even if he would go back to monotonous labor in the skyscrapers of Wall Street. The city's restlessness contrasted with his stupor as he passed businessmen energized by the fear of losing their income, knowing what they were missing in their lives.

A changed man, Alexander drifted onto his bed, knowing that he could now visit the field whenever he wanted to find peace, simply by closing his eyes.

Logan Ward

Olentangy Liberty High School

X. Walden

Walden
by Henry David Thoreau, 1854

In search of the simple life, Thoreau spent several years at Walden, a tiny cottage in the woods near Concord, Massachusetts. *Walden* is Thoreau's memoir of that time. He loved nature and devoted much of the book to his observations and musings about the natural world.

In *Walden*, Thoreau wrote, "We can never have enough of nature. We must be refreshed by the sight of inexhaustible vigor, vast and titanic features, the sea-coast with its wrecks, the wilderness with its living and its decaying trees, the thunder-cloud, and the rain which lasts three weeks and produces freshets."

(Previous Page)

Floral Beauty *by Kaitlyn Morrison*

Big Walnut High School

Leaves of Gold

The autumn swaying chilly, breaking into November winter,
Branches rattled and blunt against bark cracking and winds cold,
Stems split and crinkled, dried leaves snipped and splintered,
Through a sunset meadow, the sky flaked with leaves of gold.

Hair of gold and hazel blown soft and sweet a smell,
Skin fair and pale, cherry blush and cheeks freckled,
In the breeze made music, twisting leaves and ringing bells,
The steeples towering to points, eyes green and umber speckled.

The sun glowing amber, the clouds a burning, yellow brass,
October's harvest ending in November's coming dusk,
Noses red and chilly, filled with smells of pumpkin and grass,
Through hair soft and golden, past warm smiles the breeze does brush.

Eyes of waking morning, a face of a sleeping moon,
Green and speckled amber, her sight like twinkled gems,
Sailing about the wind like ships cast sail and strewn,
Broken free from their bonds, leaves flowing from their stems.

Tender hands held together as the clouds do mix with gold,
Swirls of the shining heavens, November's morning soon to break,
Wings of fluttered silver, feathers tickled, tucked with folds,
Fingers chilled and gentle, hands rested against warm faces.

The sun a sinking wheat field grows weary in the sky,
Pale skin gentle and cold as the day does twist to night,
Two angels peered with calmness deep into each other's eyes,
Orange the clouds in sunder, lit in flame the sun's burning light.

Together they both stood, holding each other palm in palm,
Fingers locked together as they met in a warm embrace,
Past chilly ears and golden hair, zephyrs blow cool and calm,
Wings wrapped and blanketed, warm cheeks pressed face to face.

And as the sun sank to ashes in the span of the western red maples,
Tucked behind pillowed trees, cotton-candy clouds and fluttered feathers,
Winds blowing cool, soft lips sweet under wings of hazel,
Green and setting orange, they flew into the clouds together.

Adam Willis

Hayes High School

Editor's note: Each **quatrain** (four-line stanza) of this poem
employs an elegant **alternate rhyme scheme**. This means that the
four lines of each quatrain end in alternating rhymes.

All in a Day's Troubles

Crackle. Crunch. Red, orange, and yellow float in the wind. Pine and wet earth clear my sinuses. A crisp November morning is upon me. As sounds blend together and darkness becomes daylight, that sound, snapped like a belt being whipped, wakes me up. Thick dew sticks to brown, fading grass. Chilly northern winds tickle the back of my neck. Yet here I am, frozen like a popsicle, up in a tree, for nothing more than a simple goal. Not to show manliness or to prove a point. It's okay if I go home with nothing to show. Just letting nature go by without a care in the world sparks interest in detail. Why do squirrels sound like deer? Is it? Nope, just another one storing a walnut that it will soon forget, and a tree will sprout from that seed.

Then that familiar soft step comes within earshot. With stealth like a ninja, I slowly rise up and prepare myself for the worst. Peeking over the horizon in the red and purple halos from the hazy morning sun, there's the goal, just out of reach. The king of the woods, old and wise, knows where I am, but not what I am. He keeps a careful eye on me, and I strain not to move a muscle. Carefully maneuvered feet, silent and skillful. Sweet smells of corn and minerals bring the king into my seclusion. Heart thumping like a jackhammer, I take a breath and draw.

Perpendicular to me, I squeeze my hopes into inches of carbon fiber. *Thwap*, like a nail into wood, soft yet shocking. Before I realize what happened, the woods fall quiet.

I start to shiver, not from the cold but from the adrenaline that once was controlled but is now released like a opened flood gate. Time ticks as fast as a snail crawls. Once again, the woods become busy with birds chirping, critters hopping along, and me contemplating the placement of my deed. There is no take back if a mistake had been made. Finally, that gut feeling says it's time.

Light red dots the warm colors beneath me. Stress releases in a sigh that seems to decompress the body. Dad joins me as the final step is taken, and there he lies. Just a short piece from where I waste my days according to any city slicker. I had completed the one goal I had. Learning life lessons along the way. A thank-you to the lord above and a hug from Dad, knowing he's proud of me. Even if today wasn't a success story, there was plenty to enjoy from dawn till dusk.

Trent Beach

South-Western Career Academy

Sight

It's freezing, this place shows
the symmetry of nature.
The center guarded by a being forced to stay put,
forced to stay planted.

Its limbs out and about, alone.
But, it's not alone, beings surround it,
also stuck also planted, also with no foliage,
like a man with no hair.

But further away, there is hope
there are beings who sprouted green.
Who will forever sprout green!

It's bright, the rays of the
sun give me warmth, but I can still
feel the frozen air.

Nature is once again accompanied by
man-made objects like concrete paths and
wooden seats.

It's peaceful, there is glass
But it appears not to be transparent.
Instead all that can be seen is the reflection
of fallen foliage.

This reminds me that what one sees
isn't always what is there.

Kevin Garita

South-Western Career Academy

A Winter Haiku

The snowflake falls down
Guided by the cold, dry wind
Right onto my nose

Olivia Loudon

Wellington School

Editor's note: A **haiku** is a style of unrhymed Japanese poetry composed of three lines with the syllable pattern 5-7-5. The contemplation of nature is a classic subject for a haiku.

Rain Drops

The rain drips from the sky and onto the mountaintops
It pours down, down, down
Now it's in the valley
It evaporates at some point
All those feelings and obstacles are over
It's over, right?

Perspiration

It starts all over again
You wonder how it feels to be at the top
Above the mountaintops
Over the clouds
Aloft in the heavens
Beyond anything anyone can see
Looking up in admiration

But, how would you feel when it all rushes back
When you remember
Why rain was pouring down to begin with
It feels everlasting
Maybe one day
It'll stop raining, just for one day

Erika Cruz

South-Western Career Academy

Small Moments

Morning dew glistened on my front yard like glass, as the world woke from its slumber. I wished that I could have paralleled the beauty I witnessed around me, but a measly Monday was in front of me. The book bag on my back reminded me of the work I would be giving and receiving during the day. Like most other teens, I didn't hate high school, but it was a chore.

The concrete bits on my walkway crunched beneath my feet, and three birds in the nest above me chirped rapidly, maybe begging their mother to stay with them as they watched her disappear. I left my morning view behind, as I heard the familiar screech of the school bus doors opening. My feet responded by becoming heavier, but I forced them forward.

"Chirp! Chirp! Chirp!" I heard and turned.

A hatchling was falling to the ground, trying its best to flap its young wings. I knew that it would hit the ground even if I dove for it, but my conscience conquered my logic before I could stop my body. The grass stained my new jeans while my hands reached for the blur of falling feathers. I closed my eyes and hoped that the tiny creature would land perfectly in my grasp, and everything would be okay.

"Cheep!"

I had never held wildlife in my hands, but holding that small life softened me. This delicate creature seemed to trust me. It was a baby, an older one, but a baby still. There was a streak of white along its wing, and its entire body displayed dark and light tones of gray. As a child, I had always seen birds in our tree, but I had never looked close enough to appreciate their colors.

"Hello, little one," I whispered as I stood up. The driver poked his head out the school bus door.

"Hey! You coming, kid? Now or never," he said.

I chose the latter.

The bird's eyes appeared to stare through mine while I carried the hatchling toward my porch and into the nearest azalea bush. There was plenty of cover for the baby bird, and an old nest had been left as a gift. I placed it lightly in its temporary home. The bird ruffled its feathers and sunk into the nest, filling half of the space.

Twigs and leaves covered the young bird's hiding spot. "I'll be back," I whispered. Thinking about its mother, my anxiety grew for her.

Now my problem was that there was nothing I could do. I had no time left. My walk to school was torment.

After the final school bell of the day, my feet flew me home with strong intention. My hope was clear, but my reality was uncertain. This little bird needed me, and in a weird way, I needed it too. Success was a familiar feeling, as I desired to see this bird fly from my grasp, leaving me completed.

My street sign was an arrow pointing to my destination, as my road was a treadmill. The sky was no different than that morning, shining bright and smiling back at me. I silently placed my bag on my porch, and I crept over to the bush as if I were a cat, about to pounce. My eyes locked on the empty nest. No trace of the bird. Frantically, I searched, my eyes darting every which way. My heart beat fast, and my head flooded with ideas of what might have happened while I was busy with the mundane tasks of school.

Then, a breakthrough. Overhead, the mother and two babies sliced through the air. Hope ran in my thoughts, but there was no third baby. I held back tears while holding my eyes to the sky.

"Chirp!"

Small wings flapped above me. It was behind its family, and it was flying. I held back tears and embraced the warmth in my heart. It needed me no more. The maternal instincts I hadn't known I had wanted to shelter the bird, yet it had escaped my grasp. Small success from a blunder had been won. Life would go on, and this bird flew away because of me. My hands had impacted another being. Why my hands? It didn't matter. The waves may be small, but each ripple touches the edge of the pond.

Abbey Elizondo

Bexley High School

Peace in the Rain

I find peace in the rain.

Rain and thunder are my music, my comforter, my healer. It revives me when I am weak, soothes my burns and my wounds. The soft rumbling and trickling drown out the overwhelming buzz of the world around.

Of course, there is no one around me now. I am all alone. It is only the rain and me. I relish the icy drops on my face and the wet earth beneath me. The ache in my side from a rogue bullet has numbed, and the red blood washed away, making it seem as if I was never shot. As if I wasn't dying.

I should be afraid. I should feel helpless, forsaken. But the rain calms me, whispers to me. *It won't be long now. Only a little longer, and you'll be home.* I smile softly, rain dripping into my mouth, my eyes, my hair.

The horrors of war have fled from my mind, replaced by the tranquility of this moment. There is no suffering, no crying, no agony. I lie here in silence. Forgotten by the world, cradled by the rain.

I know my time must soon come. I don't have the strength to say my farewells, but the rain carries my whispers to those I love. I will miss them, but I feel no sadness. I am ready.

As the world begins to darken around me, the rain embraces me one last time, guiding me toward a happy immortality, and I give in willingly.

Maysa Holloway

Olentangy Hyatts Middle School

Cows

Already, it was the start to a perfect morning as the rain pounded against the side of my car. I had done makeup in the car, the highway was shut down, I was late to work, and now I was navigating my way through the dimly lit side roads of the stormy countryside. My little red car wound around each bend and through field after field. Driving calmly through the storm, I was just on the way to work—and *screech!*

I slammed on the brakes as a herd of cows found their way onto the narrow road. My car slid and skidded until I stopped right before one of the cows.

It stared at me with a blank look and huffed as it made fun of my predicament. Under the long lashes, there was a spark of mocking in the pools of brown. I looked out the passenger window to see that the cows must have been looking for the greener side of the fence, because the fence that should have kept them in their barn and grazing fields was wide open from the winds of the storm. With their open door of opportunity, nothing was stopping the cows from an early morning snack, and nothing was stopping them from keeping me from getting to work for a bit of entertainment.

I honked the horn—no, sorry, I *blasted* the horn. I slammed my fist on that horn until it was my favorite instrument. It blared and howled in the rain, which was beginning to disperse. The cows only chewed more slowly on the grass on the side of the road, and the cows mooed along with the chorus of my beeping until it only caused more cows to make their way onto the road. And in reply to my clamorous song, the cows stared back at me with a blank stare.

My forehead fell onto the steering wheel and caused the horn to let out a long groan. I rolled down the window for another attempt. I called and I screamed. I found myself begging for the cows to move a bit, even a bit, so I could squeeze my little red vehicle through the sea of cows. I cried and wished, making my cruddy car-applied makeup look even cruddier. In my time of anger and frustration, I realized I had started talking to cows as if it might help me. And in reply to my small mental breakdown, the cows stared back at me with a blank stare.

As a last resort, I opened the door of my car and stood in front of the cow nearest to my door. I stared into the blank stare, the large brown eyes, the slowly munching mouth, and that slight spark of mockery.

"Please, oh please, will you move so I can get to work? Please?" I whispered to the cow's face.

My cheeks flushed red with the honest plea, and the cow's spark grew to a flame. Her eyes were no longer mocking, but they shone with a humorous glint, as though the cow finally taught her calf manners. With her head back to the sky, she let out a loud call. A low and harmonious moo, which soon echoed back from all directions. The cow sea began to part. In a feeling of bewilderment and in a bit of a daze, I realized that using the "magic word" had just worked on a cow, and I hopped back into the car. I clicked my seat belt, closed the door, and I was on my way through the roaring crowd of cows. In thanks, I waved outside my window and let out a small beep from my horn.

And as I began again on the winding country roads, I couldn't help but hear the roaring of a horn behind me, followed by beautiful shouts of frustration.

Lucy Loudon

Bishop Watterson High School

Fables for Our Time
by James Thurber, 1940

In Thurber's twisted takes on Aesop's fables, a unicorn causes marital strife, wolves accuse rabbits of making trouble (and then eat them), and a city mouse takes the wrong bus to the country. In each seemingly silly story in this collection, Thurber satirized modern life and commented on human relationships and behaviors.

The morals of his fables include such helpful advice as:
"Stay where you are. You're sitting pretty."
"He who hesitates is sometimes saved."
"There is no safety in numbers, or in anything else."

(Previous Page)

Maize *by Thessalia Stephanou*

Arts & College Preparatory Academy

Death by Nuggets

"Ready to beam up the Earth beings, everyone?" Cklevlen asked excitedly. He received many nods of confirmation—a nonverbal sign of communication they'd picked up from studying the Earth beings.

Artler lowered the ship into Earth's atmosphere, while Slewry aimed the beam.

"Look!" shouted Faln, who was watching the monitors. "We got two!"

The second they were inside, Artler blasted the ship out of the atmosphere and into Earth's orbit, where they would linger while studying the Earth beings.

Cklevlen went to retrieve the Earth beings from the chamber where they were stored. He entered with them and said, "Look! We got one of the four-legged-furry-ones! The other one is very small though; we must have gotten a child."

"It's okay," Faln said, coming over to inspect them, "It shouldn't matter that much."

Cklevlen agreed.

The four-legged-furry-one was sniffing at Cklevlen's legs, and the small one was sitting on the ground, looking around with wide eyes.

"They look confused," Artler deduced, "We should talk to them." He, being the only one who had been able to get the hang of Earth language, walked over to the small one and kneeled down. He waved, like this kind of Earth being does, and said, "Kon'nichiwa, me llamo Artler. Et toi?"

The little one reached up and grabbed Artler's waving hand.

He jumped back and looked at his hand in disgust. "Agh! It's so sticky!"

The four-legged-furry-one was now running around smelling everything, leaving hair in its wake. It let out a sound that none of them had ever heard before. It was loud and not discernible as a word. They all yelped.

With their fearful attention on the four-legged-furry-one, the small one got up onto its two pudgy legs and walked, unnoticed by the researchers, to the brightly colored control panel on the wall.

"Blue!" it said, slapping a sticky hand on a button.

The ship lurched and everyone was knocked off balance; the small Earth being toppled over completely. This got their attention. They all turned to the small one, whose face was turning bright red. It opened its mouth wide, squeezed its eyes shut, and let out a wail even worse than that of the four-legged-furry-one.

No matter what they did, it wouldn't stop wailing.

To his dismay, in the corner of the room where the four-legged-furry-one had been, Faln found a puddle of smelly, yellow liquid.

"What is this?" he yelled.

The others joined him, happy to move away from the flailing limbs of the small one.

"I think it's some sort of excretion," Cklevle

n said in disgust.

Though disgusted, something caused a wave of calm to come over the researchers. It took a moment for them to realize that this was because the small one had stopped wailing. They looked over to find that it was not where it was before. It was walking, rather unsteadily, around the room, touching *everything*.

Artler shuddered; he could only imagine how sticky all the equipment must be now.

Faln ran over to it in an attempt to stop its rampage. "It's saying something!" he yelled. "I don't know what, but it sounds like Earth language."

The small one was muttering as it grabbed something from atop Slewry's desk and put it into its mouth. It evidently didn't like it because it removed it from its mouth and threw it across the room, repeating the word. Slewry was unhappy to find that his desk toy was now covered in liquid.

"What?" Artler asked in Earth language to the small one, attempting to understand.

"Nuggets!" it shouted, stomping away.

"Do any of you know what that means?" he asked helplessly.

"NUGGETS!" it yelled again, louder this time. Its face was turning red again, which couldn't be a good sign. "NUGGETS!"

"What is 'nuggets'?" Faln asked hopelessly.

Nobody knew.

The small one ran around the room, screaming the same word, grabbing things off tables and slapping buttons, unable to be stopped by the terrified researchers. The four-legged-furry-one was similarly running around and making the same noise it did before, adding to the din.

Cklevlin looked out the window. "Guys, I don't think this is good..."

The others joined him, only to see that they were hurtling back toward Earth.

"No!" Artler shouted, running to the steering mechanism in an attempt to save them. All of the controls were hopelessly sticky and slimy with the same substance that covered Slewry's desk toy. Nevertheless, he tried everything he could, but they were moving too quickly to reroute, and Earth's gravity was pulling them in. He looked back at his friends with an expression of defeat that meant there was no hope. They were going to die to the sound of an Earth being shouting "NUGGETS!"

Abby Taggart

Upper Arlington High School

JUUL by Anthropologie: An SNL-Style Skit

CAST
FEMALE NARRATOR (not seen on camera)
WOMAN #1—late 40s
WOMAN #2—mid 40s
WOMAN #3—40s
WOMAN #4—40s
TEEN GIRL
TEEN BOY
Handful of MALE and FEMALE TEENS between the ages of 5 and 18
MALE CONSULTANT
YOUNG FEMALE MODEL—late 20s

Scene opens with WOMEN looking at clothes in Anthropologie. They are all dressed in a very fashion-forward, "Anthropologie" style. They look like women who are trying to find a way to connect with their kids, but they are dressed like they are going to brunch with other rich moms. There is playful music in the background.

NARRATOR
This holiday season, we know you're stressed
thinking about what to get your kids, nieces,
and nephews.

The WOMEN look distressed and are shaking their heads.

WOMAN #1
(Sighing and pausing from searching through clothes rack.)
Veronica has gotten harder to shop for
every year.

NARRATOR
We know you don't have time to get to know
your kids, which is why you look up "lit trends
4 teens" to get what they actually want.

Camera cuts to WOMAN #2 in a nightclub googling "lit trends 4 teens" on her iPhone.

156

> NARRATOR
> You also don't want to go to a toy store like
> the poor moms and get a plastic piece of
> trash.

Cut to WOMAN #3 in a toy store trying to control her screaming toddlers with a backpack leash.

> That's why, here at Anthropologie, we're
> releasing our new JUUL by Anthropologie.

Close-up of a JUUL by Anthropologie. It has all sorts of shells, buttons, and random pieces of fabric affixed to it

> NARRATOR
> Our new JUUL by Anthropologie is guaranteed
> a thank-you from your kid.

Cut to a 13-YEAR-OLD GIRL opening her gift of the JUUL. She embraces MOM, and they both dab.

> NARRATOR
> We personally handcraft each one, so they
> smell like our candles when you blow them
> out.

Cut to WOMAN #3 sitting at a table, peacefully smelling her lit Anthropologie candle. Then camera zooms out to her 16-YEAR-OLD SON Juuling the Anthro-JUUL. MOM and SON give each other a thumbs-up.

> NARRATOR
> Our JUUL is also styled so that you can easily
> fit it anywhere and take it on the go!

Cut to a TEEN BOY by his locker trying to jam the JUUL in his pocket, but it won't fit because of all the doodads on it.

NARRATOR

Oh, you missed our Black Friday sale? No
big deal! We sell our JUULs for only $120, so
you can save more money for our goat-hair
sweaters, am I right?

Cut to WOMAN #4 in a dressing room wearing an enormous white goat-hair sweater and checking herself out in the mirror.

NARRATOR

Scared that your kids will get addicted to
nicotine? No need to worry! That's why
there's Rehab by Nordstrom.

Background music stops. In an empty Nordstom, a group of KIDS are sitting in a circle around a white guy in a bow tie. All the children are between the ages of 5 and 18.

CONSULTANT

It's hard, I know. But that's why you're here.
We're going to get you from here *(waves hand
to gesture at the kids)* to here *(waves hand,
dramatically passing by a gorgeous live model
to gesture at a naked Nordstrom mannequin.)*

Cut to a bunch of different close-up clips of PARENTS' hands giving KIDS JUULs (one of the hands is a baby's). End with a picture of the Anthro-JUUL looking nice next to the box it comes in.

NARRATOR

Give the gift of the season because, God, you
love 'em.

(CLOSE)

McKenna Merriman

Columbus School for Girls

Editor's note: A **parody** is a humorous imitation of another piece of writing, often done in an ironic or sarcastic manner. This piece parodies the script of an advertisement for television. The long-running comedy sketch show *Saturday Night Live (SNL)* has often featured fake advertisements, including "Mom Jeans," "Bass-O-Matic," and "Taco Town."

The Gun

It was said that there hadn't been a war for 40,000 years, and man was beginning to become bored. Something had to be done. Man had ceased to be interested in peace and so required another occupation. One such man, called Deets, had an idea one day while working in the orchard.

"Start a war!" he said.

He was tired of working, drinking cider, and generally relaxing. So, the natural conclusion would be to start a war.

"But with whom?" he wondered. "I never liked Dean, that's for sure. Of course! I'll start a war with Dean!"

Dean was a man who lived about a mile away on his farm with his wife and children, who had stolen a number of pears belonging to Deets the previous fall.

"But how to do it?" said he.

He could stab them, bash their heads in, burn their house down with them still inside, or beat them to death with their own limbs. But Deets remembered something his father had told him, long ago, when Deets was very young. He had been sitting on his father's knee, and his father had said to him, as the sun set behind the mountains, "Son, if you ever meet someone, someone special I mean, someone you really want to kill, look in the barn. I assure you it would be worth your time."

So Deets, remembering the advice of that wise old man, went out to the old barn and undid the rusting padlock on the barn door. He opened it up, and sunlight flooded inside for the first time in 60 years, revealing a peculiar machine. It was large and bulky, made from black, heavy steel. It was shaped like a long cylinder that became thinner as it progressed from one end to the other, all set on two sturdy wheels. On the cylinder was written the word "GUN" leading to Deet's assumption that it was, indeed, the gun.

In the afternoon sun, Deets wheeled out the iron beast from the barn onto the lawn. After closer inspection, he discovered a cluster of papers tucked between the wheels, diagramming various components and functions of the weapon. It detailed how it was loaded, how it was fired—everything he might need to know to operate the archaic machine. It took Deets all afternoon, but by sunset, he had finished reading the instructions, so that he could easily operate the thing.

He cleaned the gun thoroughly, oiled it, polished it, and whatnot. By the end, Deets was so proud of himself that he called his wife out to see.

"Why, Deets!" said she, "It's a pretty-looking thing, but what is it?"

"It's a gun." Deets replied.

"A gun?"

"Yeah."

"What's it for?"

"I'm going to start a war."

"What in heaven are you doing that for?"

"I just felt it'd been a while since we had one."

"Well, darling, that isn't a good reason to start a war!"

"I have other reasons!"

"Like what?"

"Like killing the Deans, that's what!"

"Oh Deets..."

"What!?"

"Darling, that's a wonderful idea!"

"It is?"

"Yes! With Mr. Dean stealing our pears and whatnot, and their children stampeding through our property, and don't even get me started on Mrs. Dean! The cow!"

It took Deets all night, but eventually, with much toil, he rolled the gun to the top of the hill, aimed it toward the Dean homestead, and placed a large, metal shell into the weapon. He stood there, wiping his brow, and looked pleased at his handiwork.

He turned and saw his wife behind him, setting up two wooden folding chairs about ten feet away. Together, they sat down, looking lovingly at the gun silhouetted in the rising sun. Deets's wife, a meager smile stretching slowly like a waking cat across her face, reached into her apron and retrieved two bottles of aged cider. They sipped the drinks quietly, as they simply enjoyed the singing of the birds and the silence of each other's company.

"It's been a while since we really spent time together," Deets said.

"Well, that can't be helped sometimes," said Mrs. Deets.

"I know, but I just feel like we haven't talked much of late."

"Yes, but you're busy tending the orchard, and I manage to keep myself occupied."

"You know I love you, don't you?"

Mrs. Deets turned to him, seeming surprised. A tear brimmed in her eye.

"You haven't said that in more than a year."

They embraced on that hill for what seemed like eternity.

"Come on," Deets said, "let's kill our neighbors."

Deets looked at his wife, kissed her, fired the gun, and the Dean household went up in fire and smoke and a rain of splintered wood, all mixed with human flesh and a fine red mist. It was bliss.

Sam Horner

Homeschooled

That Little Rascal

I've got to hide it, but where? *Think, Joe, think.* He's found it in the top cupboard, behind the cleaning supplies, even on top of the fridge! That little rascal can smell them from across the house. He's quick, too—very quick. One day, I came into the kitchen to find him balancing on two chairs and three pillows, hanging precariously over the floor, just because he thought he smelled them. He broke his arm that day, but not before he cleaned out every one of them. He didn't cry once that day at the hospital. He kept reaching into his pants and coming out with another one. He must've crammed 30 in there.

Maybe I can hide it between the asparagus and the kale. He never goes near 'em. Yeah, that's what I'll do. Maybe they can mask the smell. But as I'm walking into the kitchen, there he is, sitting there waiting for me.

"Oh, uh, hey, there," I say.

He just smiles and holds out his hands. I shake my head, and the smile disappears. I know what's coming before his lip even starts to quiver. He knows he'll get me with it. It works every time.

"No, come on, just sto…"

I'm cut off by a deafening scream of agony and sorrow. It cuts through the silent air like a knife. I hope our neighbors don't call the police on us… again.

I break. You can't blame me. You just can't imagine what it's like. I break and give him two of them. He stops automatically, right away. They're gone in ten seconds, and he runs upstairs. I let out a breath. He has a problem.

I walk over to the cabinet where we keep the kale and other things like that. I open it, and there's a note.

"Hey, Dad, you thought you could hide it from me, huh? I don't think so. Yeah. Gotcha."

I just look at it for a minute. Wow. I wish he could put his cleverness to work at school. My shoulders slump, and I walk over to the table.

I set the cookie jar down and leave. I give up. He won.

Michael Newell-Dimoff

Whetstone High School

Fluffy the Special Guppy

Hi! My name is Johnny, and this is my show-and-tell for today. I want you to meet my first pet guppy—Fluffy! When I got him at the pet store two days ago, I picked him because he was just so special. Whenever I walked past the glass, he would swim right into it, *really* fast and headfirst. He would play hide-and-seek whenever I banged on the tank; sometimes, he would even flip himself over for minutes at a time and act dead! It's like whenever I was near, he showed so many signs that we were supposed to be together, that he belonged with me!

Even the worker who took him out for me said he was special! He said stuff like, "He has some health problems...we've considered giving him 'the flush,' but if you want him...then you can have him, little man!"

Of course, I squealed that I wanted him!

So, they stuffed Fluffy in a little bag, and I tossed him in the back seat. I was *so* very excited to have him! Fluffy came with beautiful purple-green scales and big bright eyes—like he's always looking for danger! My little scout! He even played that one "dead" game whenever I shook up his baggie!

When we were getting closer to our house, my mommy said that I should keep Fluffy in his makeshift home, but pour warmer tap water around it, just so he could get used to such a new "en-vir-nor-ment." Of course, I just reminded her that he was a special fish, and that he could handle anything.

Mommy whispered a joke like, "Oh dear God, I'll pray for that poor fish." I can't really remember!

When we pulled in the driveway, I hopped right out and accidentally dropped Fluffy, picked him right back up again and raced to the kitchen to give him his new forever home: my favorite cereal bowl. After all, a special fishie deserves a special habitat!

I figured he was hungry after such a long journey home, so I gave him a slice of bologna by plopping it in the bowl. What a dream that must have been for Fluffy! A bright pink sky that you can also eat?! Guppy paradise!

After I took him to my room, Fluffy still hadn't eaten his bologna, so I decided to take the slice out and play with him a little. I found him playing that game of his again! He is *just so* silly, he really is! I decided I wanted to play too, so I took him from the water, and I lay down on the carpet next to him. He flopped around a bit, which I knew meant one thing: he wanted to dance! We had fun for hours until Mommy called up that it was time for bed.

Then, I put him back in his bologna-flavored water and let him continue with his favorite game. He's kept it going since. Let's see if he's playing right now! Where is he?...Not this one...oh, found him!

Remember, friends, always check your back pocket!

This is what he looks like, everyone. I know! So purdy! Anybody want to touch him? He's not so fluffy as his name would make you think, but he sure is funny.

Wow! Look at that! He's changing color now, too! He used to be purple-green, and now he's just...green! And his eyes are super wide open; he must really be excited to see all of you!

Now, I want your ideas on this: I'm thinking of getting Fluffy a friend. Maybe...a lady friend? If I did, all three of us could play together after school every day! Or maybe I could give Fluffy to the class aquarium? What do you think, Mrs. Waterstreet? All right, good! Then you'll think about it.

In conclusion, friends: I was totally right. Fluffy is really a special guppy, and I can't wait to see what his future holds!

Evan Stefanik

Big Walnut High School

Editor's note: An **unreliable narrator** is a narrator who cannot be depended on to tell the truth. The narrator may be full of lies or delusions . . . or just may be very young and not so smart. Sometimes the reader is surprised to find out the narrator is unreliable; other times, the narrator's skewed viewpoint adds humor.

P(l)easantly Satisfied

Sweat began to accumulate on his forehead. He stood in front of the extravagant castle doors, waiting. It was over 100 degrees outside, and it felt even hotter in the arrogant sunshine. Nervously, he glanced at the green hills behind him. He wanted desperately to get inside, out of the sun. But the freedom of the open world that was so close felt so far out of his reach. It became a fixed stare out into the rolling hills. Then, a loud noise came from in front of him, making him whip his head around. The great castle doors were being opened.

Humphrey Washbuckle stepped through the extraordinarily massive entrance. Two castle guards showed no sign of emotion as they looked straight ahead, on both sides of him. They held the doors open, and he slowly walked through, with moisture running down his face. The doors shut with an uncomfortable slam behind him. Humphrey stopped to look around the room, because he had never really taken the time to.

Great white pillars held up the ceiling, which looked millions-of-men tall to him. The castle had very few windows. On the walls were paintings, which appeared to be very organized. The closest painting on the right was the first king to have lived in the castle. On the other side of the room, directly across from it, was a painting of the king's wife. As Humphrey looked down the room, he could see every royal couple, up to the most recent one.

He started to walk again. In his hands was a hot platter of the king's lunch. As he took each step, he felt like the eyes of every king and queen who had ever lived were mowing him down. Across from him, at the other side of the room, sat the king himself on his throne.

Humphrey took every step carefully, so as not to drop the platter. He made it to the king. Today, the king was wearing a golden robe, red pants, and slippers. The obese tank of a man looked down at the peasant below him. Picking at his large beard, he ordered Humphrey to kneel.

He kneeled.

With thin, shaking hands, Humphrey helplessly held out the silver platter of food. He was nothing. At this point in time, Humphrey Washbuckle felt inferior to another man.

He was not very fond of the feeling.

The king took the platter from him with greedy hands and began to eat. Humphrey stayed kneeling and stared at the marble floor. The sweat kept sliding down his nose, gravity pulling it into a puddle. Humphrey noticed it was unbearably hot in the room, not at all different from outside. As he sat there, impatiently, he began to tap his fingers on his leg. He would lift his index, then tap, then middle, then tap, then ring, then pinky. The sound of food being chewed, swallowed, chewed, swallowed, was so close, it was driving him crazy. He sat there at another man's feet, feeling useless.

Suddenly, his eyes were drawn to the king's sword. It balanced against the side of the throne, looking strong, looking elegant. It appeared to have screaming potential, just waiting to be used. He looked at the king, oblivious of his surroundings, and then back at the beautiful weapon.

The peasant leaped from his position on the floor, causing the king to be startled and throw food in the air. Humphrey grabbed the sword and stood up, making eye contact with his target. Never before had he felt so much power. The adrenaline in his veins thrust his arms forward. The blade pierced skin, muscle, and a heart.

It wasn't long before the guards did the same to Humphrey, but not soon enough to save the king. Humphrey fell to his knees, and he watched with an animalistic hunger as the king's body slid off of the throne and onto the floor with a satisfying thump.

Humphrey smiled with contentment, and blood dripped out of his mouth, infiltrating the perfect castle. His job was done.

Adam Ellis

Grandview Heights High School

An Ode to Roots

My friend says that they like you,
But I can't get behind such a lie.
A smile on their face, they are happy,
Yet only tears can be found while I cry.
You've given such joy and charity,
But I am filled to the brim with disgust.
They are beaming with pure satisfaction,
I can't fathom where they put that trust.
Your accessories seem like cheating,
Though you are twice as hated without.
I only ever seem to tolerate you
When you're flaunting those extras about.
Certain places treat you differently,
Some making me hate you even more.
High on the list to hang out with so many,
But I'd rather give you a low score.
You always feel so soft and squishy,
A highlight that could have redeemed.
However, chunks and clumps besiege you,
And I'm disappointed as my buds screamed.
You could have been something much better,
Maybe traced back to Belgian descent.
Instead you've gone too far downhill,
The makings of a tragic event.
The side that I choose when I like nothing else,
But you always manage to look like gross guck.
You make me cringe, your taste is atrocious,
Oh, mashed potatoes, why do you suck?

Bailey Rodoski
Canal Winchester High School

168

Six-Word Memoir

If you are reading this, just kidding

Haden Fulkerson

Westerville Central High School

Flip the Page

Central Ohio's Teen Literary Journal

2019

Editor: Katherine Matthews
Assistant Editor: Elizabeth Falter
Submissions Committee: Alli Aldis, Panya Bhinder, Defne Ceyhan, Kaya Ceyhan, Samantha Derksen, Abbey Elizondo, Haden Fulkerson, Sam Horner, Anna Kennedy, Allison Kuck, Grace Lawson, Olivia Loudon, Mabel Mattingly, Zizi Roberts, Diana Skestos, Julius Skestos, Abby Taggart, and Belle Walkowicz

Administrative Manager: Meg Brown
Cover Artists: Thessalia Stephanou, Julius Skestos

Publisher: Thurber House, 77 Jefferson Avenue, Columbus, OH 43215
For more copies: *Flip the Page* is available on Amazon.com.

Find us on the Thurber House website: www.thurberhouse.org
Like us on Facebook: www.facebook.com/flipthepageliteraryjournal
Follow us on Twitter: www.twitter.com/flipthepage1

Listed on the National Register of Historic Places, Thurber House (the home of humorist, author, and *New Yorker* cartoonist James Thurber during his college years) is a literary center where laughter, learning, and literature meet.

This year, on the occasion of his 125th birthday, we shall enliven James Thurber's legacy as one of the foremost humorists and cartoonists of the 20th century, for the city that raised him and the world that loves him.

During the course of the year, Thurber House, as well as other arts and culture organizations, will provide artistic experiences that celebrate Columbus arts legend James Thurber and his creative legacy as humorist, writer, and cartoonist.

Our Mission:
To celebrate the written word for the education and entertainment of the broadest possible audience and to continue James Thurber's legacy.

Thurber House is located at:
77 Jefferson Avenue,
Columbus, OH 43215

The house is a working museum open for visits from 1 pm–4 pm

Check out our website: www.thurberhouse.org

Like us on Facebook at: www.facebook.com/thurberhouse

Follow us on Twitter at: @thurberhouse

Follow us on Instagram at: @thurberhouse